"THIS WAS WRITTEN TO HELP YOU TO GROW YOUR PRACTICE. YOU MUST APPLY THE PRACTICAL ACTION STEPS TAUGHT IN THIS BOOK TO GROW YOUR PRACTICE. SEEKING PRACTICAL KNOWLEDGE WITHOUT APPLYING IT IS MEANINGLESS."

Clay Clark

(6X chart-topping podcast host, former U.S. SBA Entrepreneur of the Year for the state of Oklahoma and America's highest rated and most reviewed business coach)

"EDUCATION APPLIED IS THE KEY TO UNLOCK THE GOLDEN DOOR OF FREEDOM."

George Washington Carver

(The African American agricultural scientist and inventor who changed the world by developing powerful and game-changing methods to prevent soil depletion)

When we do not act, we subject ourselves to the plans of others. This is the current state of medicine: doctors, dentists, podiatrists, nurse practitioners, nurse anesthetists, etc. produce the value in medicine. Yet they are not allowed a "seat at the table" because they lack business training. Why? I have my conspiratorial beliefs. Regardless, I am here to empower medical providers to take back their lives through teaching the proven best-practices and the strategies being implemented by top earning medical professionals, and in the process I also look to improve medicine. Welcome to the business school you should have gotten during your medical training.

 - Dr. Timothy Johnson

"VISION WITHOUT EXECUTION IS HALLUCINATION."

Thomas Edison

(Inventor of the modern light bulb, recorded audio and recorded video)

YOU MUST CHOOSE TO LEARN FROM MENTORS OR BY MISTAKES BY DEFAULT

If you want to transform your career and the medical care you provide, you must not settle for mediocrity. You must commit yourself to winning. I want you to win. Your patients want you to win. However, to win, you have to grow. To grow, you have two options. You could spend years learning these SUCCESS SYSTEMS through traditional and expensive means, as I did. You could exhaustively read hundreds of pages of the Harvard Business Review, as I did. You could invest thousands of hours reading the autobiographies of the world's most successful people, as I did. You could even invest years and countless hours reaching out to the world's most successful people to convince them to become your business mentor, as I did. You could drag yourself and your family to expensive mindset-changing and up-sell focused seminars, as I did. My friend, you could even sprint through the minefield of business as a highly motivated idiot just as I once did while trying to convince my wife that I was learning through trial and error.

However, you could invest the time needed to read this book and implement the proven strategies found within it. If you do, I GUARANTEE you financial success and massive quantities of time freedom. The proven strategies, systems, tools, workshops, training videos and templates found within this book and at Thrivetimeshow.com WILL transform your career and the medical care you provide your patients. The choice is yours – learn from me or learn from your mistakes.

-Clay Clark

Contents

....

"The success I seek is not about buying things we don't need and can't afford. Success is about earning the financial capacity to buy back your time so that you can invest the 1,440 minutes we are all gifted everyday spending time doing things we love and with the people we actually like being around."

- *Clay Clark*

PREFACE: WHAT ARE YOU
ACTUALLY GOING TO LEARN?

In this powerful book, Clay Clark, host of the iTunes chart-topping Thrive Time Show podcast and 2007 U.S. Small Business Administration Entrepreneur of the Year for the state of Oklahoma will show you how to overcome the obstacles, limiting beliefs, and system failures that nearly every doctor encounters along the way in route to starting and growing a business. In this book, you will learn:

» How to build a duplicable and scalable business model capable of working without you.

» How to enhance (systematically) each aspect of your business to greatly reduce costs and to dramatically increase profits.

» How to build systems that are scalable and sellable (meaning that somebody else would actually want to buy your business someday).

» How to discover your company's hidden opportunities and lowest hanging fruit for quick growth.

» How to enhance both the cash flow and workflow of your business.

ARE YOU GOING TO USE A GPS OR SPEND YOUR TIME BEING CHRONICALLY LOST?

This book provides you with a step-by-step guide that will serve as your virtual business GPS and navigation system. Before global positioning systems were on every smartphone, I used to get lost. I would occasionally run into Yoda and every other wise hermit living on the outskirts of humanity. But when GPS became readily available, I had a choice. Would I allow billion-dollar, precise and proven satellite technology to guide me to my desired destinations, thus reducing my pain and expediting success? Or would I remain in a perpetual state of "jackassery?" I chose to commit myself to "jackassery" for six more months. Then, finally after much lost time, I started using a GPS when my sanity was called into question. You have that same choice today. Will you follow a proven system or will you allow the wealth-repelling force known as "jackassery" to control both you and your medical practice? Visit: www.Thrive15.com/YourBusinessSystems.

INTRODUCTION

Today I am known as the founder of DJConnection.com, the founder of EpicPhotos.com, the co-founder of EITRLounge.com, the founder of MakeYourLifeEpic.com, the former U.S. Small Business Administration's Entrepreneur of the Year for the state of Oklahoma, a writer for Entrepreneur.com, and I have been featured in *Fast Company, Forbes,* and *Bloomberg.*

However, I am actually a man-bear-pig who grew up in and out of poverty. I had to take both Algebra and the ACT three times just to get into college. My friend, if I can do this, you can too; and I am excited to show you how.

The word "poverty" means different things to different people. Having traveled around the world, I have unfortunately met people who do not have access to clean drinking water and who live permanently outside in the elements permanently. However growing up, my family was what I would call "American poor."

- Clay Clark

Definition Magician:
Poverty – "pov-er-ty" – The state of being extremely poor.

We were not homeless, but only because of the generosity of countless family and friends who wanted to help my mom and dad because they were good people with integrity. As a kid, I remember numerous times when somebody else paid our bills or provided us with clothes. I remember when my father, then in his late 30s, delivered pizzas to provide for our family rather than to just accept government assistance.

I remember growing up without money and stuttering. I remember the kids taunting me on the school bus and I remember feeling helpless. I remember making up stories and outright lies about what my dad did for a living to defend him in some way. I remember repeatedly thinking to myself, "Someday you morons are going to be poor too and when you are, I will be glad." - *Clay Clark*

"YOU MUST WALK TO THE BEAT OF A DIFFERENT DRUMMER. THE SAME BEAT THAT THE WEALTHY HEAR. IF THE BEAT SOUNDS NORMAL, EVACUATE THE DANCE FLOOR IMMEDIATELY! THE GOAL IS TO NOT BE NORMAL, BECAUSE AS MY RADIO LISTENERS KNOW, NORMAL IS BROKE."

Dave Ramsey

(The *New Your Times* best-selling author,
national radio talk show host, and financial expert)

Fast-forward to my middle school and high school years. My family moved from Oklahoma to Minnesota so my mom could go to work with her sister. However, we still never had money in the budget for the things I wanted. So I started selling gum and candy out of my locker in middle school.

Our principal (I believe his name was Mr. Johnson, no relation to Dr. Tim) eventually banned the use of gum at school and thus I quickly learned about the Law of Supply and Demand. Because it was essentially illegal to have gum and candy, now everyone wanted it and I was the "go-to guy." I made thousands of dollars selling gum and candy and I eventually moved into the t-shirt selling game. Our local high school only sold lame, soulless, and politically correct t-shirts that were approved by our athletic department, so I started producing shirts that really captured the soul of the student body. I produced t-shirts that taunted our opponents and that the students actually wanted to buy. To produce the shirts for which I had already taken orders, I had to learn all about *Adobe* Photoshop, t-shirts, heat presses, inventory management, order forms, and cash management.

NOTABLE QUOTABLE

"YOU CANNOT CONNECT THE DOTS LOOKING FORWARD. YOU CAN ONLY CONNECT THEM LOOKING BACKWARD. SO YOU HAVE TO TRUST THAT THE DOTS WILL SOMEHOW CONNECT IN YOUR FUTURE. YOU HAVE TO TRUST IN SOMETHING — YOUR GUT, DESTINY, LIFE, KARMA, WHATEVER."

Steve Jobs

(Co-founder of Apple, the founder of
NeXT and the former CEO of Pixar)

Fast-forward to 1999. I was a non-Christian believer (at the time), and yet I still decided to attend a private Christian college called Oral Roberts University because it was as far away from my parents as I could get, and it was based in my home town that I lived in until I was 12 years old (Tulsa, Oklahoma). Oral Roberts University is the alma mater for such notables as Homer Simpson's neighbor, Ned Flanders, Kathie Lee Gifford (of Regis and Kathie Lee and the Today Show), and the Grammy Award winning recording artist Ryan Tedder (frontman for OneRepublic, songwriter for Adele, Beyoncé, U2, and producer for NBC's musical competition series, *Songland*). The school was named for its charismatic and Pentecostal televangelist founder, Oral Roberts. During my time at ORU, I quickly discovered that approximately 90% of the expensive and loan-funded college courses had no practical application to your life and that attempting to pay your own way through college is very tough.

NOTABLE QUOTABLE

"START WHERE YOU ARE, WITH WHAT YOU HAVE. MAKE SOMETHING OF IT AND NEVER BE SATISFIED."

George Washington Carver

(The famous inventor who was born into slavery and who went on to invent countless uses for peanuts and sweet potatoes, which empowered millions of poor families who then grew these crops for food and a sustainable income)

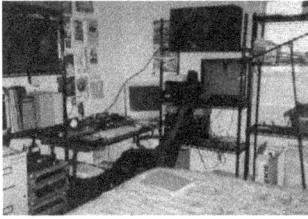

In order to pay my way through college, I started a company called www. DJConnection.com. I carried around a backpack full of flyers. I shoved these promotional flyers underneath the doors of each and every college student three times before each event. I held these events at the local Marriott Hotel located at the corner of 71st and Lewis in Tulsa, within walking distance for most of the student body.

NOTABLE QUOTABLE

"THE WAY TO GET STARTED IS TO QUIT TALKING AND BEGIN DOING."

Walt Disney

(An American entrepreneur, animator, voice actor, and film producer. He was prominent within the American animation industry and famous throughout the world, and is regarded as an American cultural icon)

I did not have a business license to promote these events. I did not have the proper insurance in place to house over 500 people in one place at one time. I did not own any of my own DJ equipment... I did not even know how to properly operate the DJ equipment. But I had nothing to lose, so I made up for it by obsessing about producing incredible events that people loved to attend. I grew the business to the point that we were actually providing entertainment for thousands of events per year (as many as 80 events on many weekends) before I decided to sell the company so that I could move on to the investor and business coaching phase of my life.

Since selling www.DJConnection.com, I have started many successful ventures (www.EITRLounge.com, www.EpicPhotosTulsa .com, and www.MakeYourLifeEpic.com, just to name a few) and have coached thousands of business owners through the process of developing the duplicable and scalable best-practice business systems necessary for sustainable growth. In fact, I will list the actual growth of my actual clients during the year 2019. Through the years, I have spent the majority of my working hours in conference rooms, workshops, and on stage at public speaking events. However, when my son was born blind and my dad lost the ability to use his arms and legs, the ability to feed himself, and even the ability to breathe on his own from

Parkinson's, it became increasingly clear to me that my time on this planet is very limited and that I must teach these provable systems to people like you, as soon as possible that you can start enjoying the benefits of time and financial freedom ASAP. PBS, CNN Money, and countless news outlets have reported that half of U.S. adults no longer believe in the "American Dream". This is why I feel like I have a lot of work to do. - Clay Clark

Accolade Exteriors
Stuart Weikel
www.AccoladeExteriors.com
2018 - 2019 Up 80%

Amy Baltimore, CPA
Amy Baltimore
www.AmyBaltimoreCPA.com
2018 - 2019 Up 34%

Angel's Touch
Christina Nemes
www.CapeCodAutoBodyandDetailing.com
2018 - 2019 Up 71%

Back to Basics Builders
Joe Burbey
www.HomeRemodelingMilwaukee.com
2018 - 2019 Up 41%

Barbee Cookies
Kat Graham
www.BarbeeCookies.com
2014 - 2015 Up 140%

Best Buy Window Treatment
Ergun Aral
www.BestBuyWindowTreatments.com
2018 - 2019 Up 76%

Bigfoot Restoration
Marc Lucero & Stephen Small
www.BigFootRestoration.com
2018 - 2019 Up 26%

Bogard and Sons Construction
Andy Bogard
www.BogardandSons.com
2018 - 2019 Up 32%

Breakout Creative
Chris De Jesus
www.BreakOutCreativeCompany.com
Up 59% Total

Brian T. Armstrong Construction
Incorporated
Brian T. Armstrong
www.BrianTArmstrongConstructionInc.com
2018 - 2019 Up 52%

Chaney Construction
Jim and Amy Chaney
www.ChaneyConstructionTX.com
2018 - 2019 Up 19%

Colaw Fitness
Charles and Amber Colaw
www.ColawFitness.com
2018 - 2019 Up 15%

Complete Carpet
Nathan & Toni Sevrinus
www.CompleteCarpetTulsa.com
2017 - 2019 Up 298%

CT Tech
Christopher Tracy
www.CTTec.com
2018 - 2019 Up 77%

Custom Automation Technologies
Incorporated
Dan Hoehnen
www.CustomAutomationTech.com
2018 - 2019 Up 16%

D&D Custom Homes
Dave Tucker
www.MidSouthHomeBuilder.com
2018 - 2019 Up 45%

Da Vinci
Josh Fellman and Jerome Garrett
www.500KMSP.com
2018 - 2019 Up 1,097%

Delricht Research
Tyler and Rachel Hastings
www.DelrichtResearch.com
2018 - 2019 Up 300%

Dr. Breck Kasbaum Chiropractor
Dr. Breck Kasbaum
www.DrBreck.com
2018 - 2019 Up 50%

Duct Armor
Tim Borgne
www.H2OasisFloatCenter.com
2015 - 2016 Up 20%

EnviZion Insurance
Austin Grieci
www.EZInsurancePlan.com
2018 - 2019 Up 800%

Full Package Media
Thomas James Crosson
www.FullPackageMedia.com
2018 - 2019 Up 15%

Gable's Excavating Incorporated
Levi Gable
www.GEI-USA.com
2018 - 2019 Up 63%

The Garage
Roy Coggeshall
www.TheGarageBA.com
2018 - 2019 Up 33%
2017 - Present Up 70%

The Grill Gun
Bob Healey
www.GrillBlazer.com
From Idea to Manufactured Product
8,725 Funders

Raised $920,009.00 Crowd Funding the
Invention
H2Oasis Float Center
Debra Worthington
www.H2OasisFloatCenter.com
Up 17% Total

HealthRide
Ryan Graff
www.HealthRideTulsa.org
2018 - 2019 Up 10%

Healthworks Chiropractic
Jay Schroeder
www.HealthworksChiropractic.net
2018 - 2019 Up 24%

Hood and Associates CPA's, PC
Paul Hood
www.HoodCPAs.com
2018 - 2019 Up 61%

The Hub Gym
Luke Owens
www.TheHubGym.com
2018 - 2019 Up 66.38%

Inspired Spaces
Josh Fellman and Jerome Garrett
www.InspiredSpacesOK.com
2018 - 2019 Up 40%

Jean Briese
www.JeanBriese.com
2018 - 2019 Up 90%

Kelly Construction Group
Jon Kelly
www.KellyConstructionGroup.com
2018 - 2019 Up 38%

Kona Honu
Byron Kay
www.KonaHonuDivers.com
2018 - 2019 Up 14%

Kvell Fitness & Nutrition
Brett Denton
www.KvellFit.com
2018-2019 Up 35%+

Lake Martin Mini Mall
Jason Lett
www.LakeMartinCubed.com
2018 - 2019 Up 13%

Laundry Barn
Josh Fellman
www.TheLaundryBarn.com
2018 - 2019 Up 100%

Living Water Irrigation
Josh Wilson
www.LivingWaterIrrigationOK.com
2017 - 2019 Up 600%

Metal Roof Contractors
Doug Yarholar
www.MetalRoofContractorsOK.com
2018 - 2019 Up 14%

Mod Scenes
Steven Hall
www.ModScenes.com
2018 - 2019 Up 83%

Morrow, Lai and Kitterman Pediatric
Dentistry
Dr. Mark Morrow, Dr. April Lai, and Dr.
Kerry Kitterman
www.MLKDentistry.com
2018 - 2019 Up 42%

Multi-Clean
Kevin Thomas
www.MultiCleanOK.com
2018 - 2019 Up 14%

Oxi Fresh
Jonathan Barnett
Matt Kline - Franchise Developer
www.OxiFresh.com
2007 to 2019 - 400 Locations Opened

Pappagallo's Pizza
Dave Rich
www.Pappagallos.com
2018 - 2019 Up 15%

Platinum Pest
Jennifer and Jared Johnson
www.PlatinumPestandLawn.com
2018-2019 - 25% Growth
2017-2018 - 43% Growth

PMH OKC
Randy Antrikan
www.PMHOKC.com
2018 - 2019 Up 70%

Precision Calibration
Nathan Saylor
www.PrecisionCalibrations.com
2018 - 2019 Up 62%

Quality Surfaces
John Cook
www.QualitySurfacesln.com
2018 - 2019 Up 76%

Revitalize Medical Spa
Lindsey Blankenship and Crista Hobbs
www.RevitalizeMedicalSpa.com
2018 - 2019 Up 36%

Scotch Construction
Tim Scotch
www.ScotchConstruction.com
2017 - 2019 Up 492%

Shaw Homes
Aaron Antis
www.ShawHomes.com
2018 - 2019 Up 116%

Sierra Pools
Cody Albright
www.SierraPoolsandSpas.com
2017 - 2019 Up 309%

Snow Bear Air
Daniel Ramos
www.SnowBearAir.com
2018 - 2019 Up 41%

Spurrell & Associates Chartered Professional Accountants
Josh Spurrell
www.Spurrell.ca
2018 - 2019 Up 50%

Tip Top K9
Ryan and Rachel Wimpey
www.TipTopK9.com
1 Location - 10 Locations

Trinity Employment
Cory Minter
www.TrinityEmployment.com
2018-2019 Up 35%

Turley Solutions & Innovations
Rance Turley
www.TSI.lc
2018 - 2019 Up 300%

Tuscaloosa Ophthalmology
Doctor Timothy Johnson
www.TTownEyes.com
2018 - 2019 - Up 16%

Veteran Home Exterior
James Peterson
www.VeteranHomeExterior.com
2018 - 2019 Up 145%

Williams Contracting
Travis Williams
www.Will-Con.com
2018 - 2019 Up 33%

Witness Security
Keith Schultz
www.WitnessLLC.com
2017 - 2019 Up 300%

"DESIRE IS THE KEY TO MOTIVATION, BUT IT
IS THE DETERMINATION AND COMMITMENT
TO UNRELENTING PURSUIT OF YOUR GOAL, A
COMMITMENT TO EXCELLENCE, THAT WILL ENABLE
YOU TO ATTAIN THE SUCCESS YOU SEEK."

Mario Andretti

(Retired Italian American world champion racing driver, one of
the most successful Americans in the history of the sport. He and
Dan Gurney are the only two drivers to win races in Formula One,
IndyCar, World Sportscar Championship and NASCAR)

My friend, this can be your year and your time to thrive. However, YOU must commit to learning the proven systems, processes, controls, and strategies necessary to transform your big visions into reality. Once you learn and implement these systems, you will find yourself enjoying more time and freedom by owning a company that is both fun to own and operate. Sign the commitment letter below and you will begin to notice your life changing for the better.

I _____ (first and last name) commit to dedicating myself to investing the time needed to learn and implement the proven business systems and strategies in my own life and business.

Signature: _____ Date: _____

For accountability, take a picture of this signed page and email it to us at info@ThrivetimeShow.com. - Clay Clark

Quick disclaimer: For your overall benefit, I have filled this book with 100% true examples and case studies taken from my work with real clients, real families, and real healthcare professionals like you. However, to protect the privacy and confidentiality of Thrivers all around the world, I have changed a few of the identifiers (names, genders, industries, and locations). Nevertheless, these are still 100% fact-based stories. - Clay Clark

2.2

A QUICK SUMMARY OF THIS BOOK

This book was written to help you achieve massive, quick, and sustainable growth. However, if you really do wish to greatly enhance your life, your business, and both your financial freedom and time freedom, you must take the actions prescribed in this book, which are separated into four phases below. - Clay Clark

Phase 1:

Decrease Your Business's

Reliance Upon You

In order to build these world-class and duplicable systems, I must reeducate you. You have to decrease your business's reliance on you. The first portion of the book will show you why. I will provide you with the practical tools, downloadables, and templates that you will need along the way. However, you must commit to taking the action steps needed to turn your dreams into reality. - Clay Clark

Phase 2:

Unlock Your Company's Fast and
Sustainable Growth Potential by Listening
to Your Patients

....

During this portion of the book, I will show you how to identify the low-hanging fruit and the sustainable growth potential that is currently hidden within your own business, simply by listening to your current customers.

Phase 3:

Take the Limiters Off of Your Growth

....

Here I will teach you to quickly identify and eliminate the actual barriers, limiting beliefs, and systems that are causing your business to become stuck or to grow at a very slow annual growth rate.

Phase 4:
Optimize Your Personal Happiness
and Personal Life Satisfaction

....

During this phase of the book, I will teach you to optimize your quality of life so you are eager to start each day because you know it will be a day filled with meaning and purpose. Unfortunately, I have worked with thousands of clients all over the world who have earned copious amounts of money, but who enjoy very little time freedom and satisfaction with their overall quality of life. This does not have to be your reality.

NOTE: You can watch video testimonials from thousands people just like you who have gone from surviving to thriving as a result of implementing the proven strategies, systems and processes found within this book at www. ThriveTimeShow.com/Testimonials. Regardless of what industry you are in, the proven processes and strategies that we have the capacity to teach you will change your life.

"When we started, if you put my name in exactly spelled correctly, you might've found me on 20 pages back. So, we started from scratch and now we're climbing the Google search engine each day. That's a nice, new thing. People come in and are like, "Hey, I saw you online. Literally, from a year and a half ago to now, we're up double."

Dr. Breck Kasbaum
(Founder of Dr. Breck Kasbaum Chiropractor - See
his success at www.DrBreck.com)

When you mniachally obsess about wowing each
and every customer the awards will come.

....

SBA
U.S. Small Business Administration
Your Small Business Resource

Oklahoma District Office
301 NW 6th Street, Suite 116 · Oklahoma City, OK 73102 · 405-609-8000 · (fax) 405-609-8990

February 21, 2007

Mr. Clayton Thomas Clark
DJ Connection Tulsa, Inc.
8900 South Lynn Lane Road
Broken Arrow, Oklahoma 74102

Dear Mr. Clark:

Congratulations! You have been selected as the **2007 Oklahoma SBA Young Entrepreneur of the Year.** On behalf of the U.S. Small Business Administration (SBA), I wish to express our appreciation for your support of small business and for your contributions to the economy of this State.

In recognition of your achievement, **an awards luncheon will be held Tuesday, May 22, 2007** at Rose State College in Midwest City, Okla. The luncheon is sponsored by the Oklahoma Small Business Development Center. Two complimentary luncheon tickets have been reserved for you and one guest.

Arrangements for the luncheon are still being finalized. You will be notified of the details as soon as they became available. You are encouraged to bring family, friends, and business associates. Upon presentation of your award, you will have the opportunity to make acceptance comments.

Also, for our awards brochure, please email an electronic photo of yourself to darla.booker@sba.gov by Friday, March 16.

Again, congratulations on your outstanding accomplishment.

Sincerely,

Dorothy (Dottie) A. Overal
Oklahoma District Director

"We have been using Clay's Coaching and have grown exponentially. Some of the things I love about working with them is that they hold me accountable. We have set up systems in the business that make my life easier, allow me time freedom, and financial rewards. We went from owning 3 locations in 2016 to eight locations and still growing . The training we're receiving is invaluable and we hope to continue to grow with your help."

Jennifer Allen
Body Central Physical Therapy
www.BodyCentral.net

"We have increased our revenue by over 300% in less than a year! Clay has helped us with every aspect of our business from hiring, training, marketing, accounting, and has given us the practical steps to continually improve our operations. He has held us accountable, made us better leaders, and I would recommend them to any business owner or entrepreneur."

Tyler and Rachel Hastings
Delricht Research, Co-Founders of Delricht Research
www.DelrichtResearch.com

"Clay and his team provide the services that help us to get more patients into my business. They help me get the message out that I am the best orthodontist in Tulsa. They get the word out through social media and Google optimization. They helped me to create that bond with referring doctors. Nothing is too big for Clay and his staff!"

Dr. Joseph Lai
Co-owner of Kirkpatrick and Lai Orthodontics
www.KLOrtho.com

"We have gone into overdrive to get the team trained. We have had a record month!! We have collected $60,000. We have quite a bit of pending insurance as well. Cannot wait to finish all the numbers!! That is awesome! Thank you, Clay, for all that you do! We had over 30 leads in March alone!"

Jennifer Cushman
Office Manager
Face & Body Cosmetic Surgery and Medical Spa
www.FaceandBody.net

"In terms of our website, we weren't even on Google and now we are the top in Google search results. Already 70 kids signed up for camp. Could have 80-90 before it is over. The site really gives us a big time look. I am happy with it."

Don Calvert
Founder of Score Basketball
ScoreBBall.com

"We were able to move to the top of Google searches in the competitive mortgage Internet search category, we got featured on the news twice and we closed nearly 35% more loans within the first six months. The contact management system, search engine strategy and PR system you set up are producing results."

Adnan Sheikh
Founder | President
ZFG Mortgage | www.ZFGMortgage.com

"Wow. Wow. Wow. Thank you for your input and for working so hard for me behind the scenes while we were back and forth for this (for the TV show, "*The Voice*"). I am humbled and overwhelmed with gratitude. So glad to know you and your sweet family. Thanks for believing in me!"

Amanda Preslar
Founder of PreslarMusic.com

"So far we have generated $63,600 of additional annual gross revenue as a result of the ACCESS plan you helped us create. We are closing in on $10K in monthly revenue. I just signed up an additional ACCESS client and it is the 2nd one that I have landed in the last 30 days from LinkedIn. And the only thing I am doing on LinkedIn is the Myth versus Law and the Legal Mumbo Jumbo. I am not doing any other activity. So that appears to really be working in that medium. So I am making $850 a month off of my free LinkedIn subscription. I just wanted to let you know that what we are doing is working."

Scott Reib
Attorney at Law
ReibLaw.com

"Hi Clay. You have no idea how you blessed me with our conversation and the book recommendations. We have now about 20 employees working on three different construction sites. The principles in the books you recommended and the ones I 'caught' during our conversation have helped me a lot! I often tell my wife: 'If Clay Clark can run five businesses, then why cannot I run a business and a ministry?' You have been an inspiration! Thanks my friend!"

Rubens Cunha
Brazilian Missionary
www.gga.global

"I thought when I opened my clinic that I could do this all myself. I do not need additional outside help. I went to medical school. I can figure this out. But it was a very steep learning curve. Clay helped us weather the storm. He was instrumental with the specific written business plan. He's been instrumental in hiring good employees and generating our in-bound patient leads. He helped me in securing the business loans, designing our logo and branding, and in building Revolution Health. "

Dr. Chad Edwards
Founder of Revolution Health
www.RevolutionHealth.org

"Clay is a force to be reckoned with. He is a contagious, mind-expanding, 'get off your blessed assurance' motivating business coach that is positively changing my world and soon to be the whole world. Since working with Clay we've grown from a startup to a $100k + per month business."

Tim Redmond, CEO
Redmond Growth Initiatives
www.RedmondGrowth.com

"Clay, I just want you to know that this last year has been unbelievable. I have gone from poverty thinking to just a small measure of wealth thinking and, as the book said, the universe has discovered me!!! I have never felt so free! I truly have become what T. Harv Eker calls, 'a money magnet'! And it is only the beginning. We have seven revenue streams now and each of them are growing and contributing daily. Thank you Clay Clark! My life is expanding and you have been a major influence on me!"

Clay Staires
Professional Speaker/Trainer and Growth Expert
The Leadership Initiative
www.claystaires.com

"Last August we had 114 new patients compared to this August where we've had 180 patients. The system works."

Doctor April Lai
Co-owner of MLK Dentistry
www.MLKDentistry.com

....

"In just four months our internet leads have grown 12-fold."

Aaron Antis
The marketing director of Shaw Homes who has sold
over $800,000,000 of homes throughout his career.
www.ShawHomes.com

....

"Through Clay's new marketing system we have seen a marked increase in the number of patients that we are seeing every month, year over year. One month, as an example, we went from 110 new patients the previous year, to over 180 new patients in the same month. Overall growth is about 40-42% increase."

Dr. Mark Morrow
Co-founder of MLKDentistry.com

....

The
DOCTORPRENEUR

The Best Business & Medical Marketing Book

in the World for Healthcare Providers

19 18 17 16   10 9 8 7 6 5 4 3 2 1

The Doctorpreneur: The Best Business Book in the
World for Healthcare Providers
ISBN:
Copyright © 2020 by Clay Clark

Clay Clark Publishing
Published by Clay Clark
1100 Suite #100 Riverwalk Terrace
Jenks, OK 74037

The
Doctorpreneur

The Best Business & Medical Marketing Book
in the World for Healthcare Providers

Clay Clark
with
Dr. Timothy Johnson, MD

Phase #1

2.1

DECREASING YOUR BUSINESS' RELIANCE
UPON YOU

"Personally, I feel overwhelmed. I started my own business so that I could be in control of my schedule, but at the end of the day I feel like I am being held hostage by my business and the terrorists who work there. If you can show me the systems and a proven path, I will make it happen. I just need to know where to start."

-Business Owner / New Thrive15.com Member during their free one-on-one coaching session

---

NOTABLE QUOTABLE

"No one lives long enough to learn everything they need to learn starting from scratch. To be successful, we absolutely, positively have to find people who have already paid the price to learn the things that we need to learn to achieve our goals."

Brian Tracy

(Bestselling author and world-renowned speaker)

Years ago I met with a 60-year-old Texan exhausted from his soccer coaching business. He attended college on a full-scholarship as a Division 1 athlete. After graduation, he just attracted business. However, as his business grew, his physical body deteriorated from years of hard use and natural aging. Unable to personally demonstrate every drill first-hand, this coach relied on younger coaches to teach the kids the moves, drills, and systems that he had spent a lifetime creating. Furthermore, he now faced competition from another coaching facility in town.

At our first meeting we conducted our standard 13-Point Business Self-Evaluation. And it indicated that his business had many problems (or "opportunities for growth"), including:

1. He lacked any turnkey marketing systems.

2. He lacked any proven turnkey advertisements.

3. He lacked any formalized inbound sales scripts, pre-written emails, or sales presentation processes.

4. He lacked an outbound sales call script.

5. He lacked a formalized up-selling / cross-selling script.

6. He lacked a systematic customer "wow experience" baked into his workflow. He lacked any documented workflow at all.

7. He did not know his break-even point, his goal achievement point, tax deadlines, and weekly profits and losses.

8. He had no concept of his overall profitability per customer.

9. He lacked a cause-based marketing or public relations campaign.

10. He lacked any file organization or nomenclature rules in place.

11. He did not have proven processes in place for employee recruitment, job posting, and employee on-boarding.

12. He lacked an ongoing training program in place for his staff.

13. He was not being intentional about developing banking relationships or friendships with potential investors.

14. He was not intentionally leading his employees.

15. He lacked a management, follow-up, and delegation system.

16. He lacked a system in place to motivate himself and keep himself engaged and excited about the vision of his company.

17. He lacked a time management system to block out distractions and to create time to focus on the important aspects of his business.

18. His overall growth was stagnant.

19. He was behind in many of his financial responsibilities.

20. He did have a proof of concept and knew that people were willing to pay for professional soccer coaching.

21. He lacked any documented processes indicating how the company

would eventually scale (expand rapidly) to different markets.

22. He lacked financial peace, and in fact, was actually quite stressed out financially most of the time.

23. He lacked any formalized goals for his life in the areas of Faith, Family, Finances, Fitness, Friendships, and Fun.

24. He lacked any formalized or accurate checklists in place so all employee and customer questions were directed to him.

25. He did not have clarityvoice.com installed on his phone system so he was unable to hold employees accountable.

26. He had very little documentation for anything including his passwords, processes, the service experience delivery, the bathroom cleaning checklists, and the coaching process itself.

27. He lacked customer relationship management software in place, despite having worked with over 10,000 paying customers throughout his 30-year career.

This incredible man was a loyal father, a committed husband, and an outstanding coach. But he was way down the "Proven Path to Small Business Death" which includes:

1. Running out of health.   3. Running out of time.
2. Running out of money.

I am proud to say that within just four years after our first meeting, he had made SIGNIFICANT improvements in 25 of the 29 areas of weakness and became financially free. Recently he, unfortunately, had to have another surgery. But this time his team of employees and staff of coaches were prepared, trained, and ready to fill in for their mentor and leader. My friend, have you wondered why only a few entrepreneurs seem to be able to move from one successful venture to another while most business owners seem unable to find the magic formula?

Why do some college basketball coaches seem to win everywhere they go, while others just cannot seem to replicate this success? Over the years I have had the opportunity to become friends with the legendary Hall of Fame Division 1 college basketball coach, Eddie Sutton, who took four schools to the NCAA Tournament and both Arkansas and Oklahoma State to the Final Four. During his career, he was one of only eight college basketball coaches to win over 800 games. That was because he knew HOW TO WIN. No matter where Eddie Sutton coached, he was going to win because he knew the methodology, the resources, the systems, the processes, and the priorities needed to win.

NOTABLE QUOTABLE

"RESOURCES ARE WHAT HE USES TO DO IT, PROCESSES ARE HOW HE DOES IT, AND PRIORITIES ARE WHY HE DOES IT."

Clayton M. Christensen

(The legendary Harvard Business school professor
and former ThrivetimeShow.com guest)

My friend, you must become like one of these legendary coaches. YOU MUST LEARN THAT THE PARALLELS AND COMMON DENOMINATORS FOUND IN RUNNING MOST BUSINESSES FAR OUTWEIGH THE DIFFERENCES OF EACH BUSINESS TYPE AND INDUSTRY. For example, one of my clients now owns a sushi bar, a neurological center, a testosterone clinic, a cosmetic surgery business, and a liquor store. What do all these businesses have in common?

They all allow him to exchange goods and services for the monetary compensation he seeks.

Repeat after me: Medicine is no different than any other business. Now say it again, out loud! Medicine is no different than any other business. In medicine, as in any other business, entrepreneurship requires consistent application of effort to implement a proven set of strategies, proven plans, and game-changing action steps. The great entrepreneurs implement these lessons and their wallets are much bigger as a result.

NOTABLE QUOTABLE

"MOST ENTREPRENEURS ARE MERELY TECHNICIANS WITH AN ENTREPRENEURIAL SEIZURE. MOST ENTREPRENEURS FAIL BECAUSE YOU ARE WORKING IN YOUR BUSINESS RATHER THAN ON YOUR BUSINESS."

Michael Gerber

(Bestselling author of the *E-Myth* book series)

For your benefit, I need for you to take the following pledge:

I, _____, believe that although my medical practice does have unique variables and specialized aspects, the similarities of successful businesses greatly outweigh their differences. I realize that saying, "Yes, but my type of business is very different" is not helpful and is a limiting belief.

Signed: _____ Date: _____

Refusing to implement the proven systems that we will teach you during this book would be a lot like a super small Division 1 athletic director telling Hall of Fame basketball coach Coach, Eddie Sutton that he could not possibly help his team or his program to win more games because he had only coached at Creighton, Arkansas, Kentucky, and Oklahoma State, and this athletic director's school is "unique".

My friend, if you believe this mindset, you need to get one of those police-grade tasers and unleash it on your own inner thigh during a church service because that would be dumb. But it would be less dumb than working 80 hours per week in your business because you believe that you are the only one on the planet who can possibly do everything that needs to be done in the practice.

Unless you are Nick Saban, the greatest college football coach of all time, you can teach people to do your job. It is hard to teach people to become the greatest basketball coach of all time. But it is not hard to create the checklists and scripts needed for your receptionist to competently manage your office.

- Dr. Timothy Johnson

3.2

COULD YOU TAKE A VACATION FOR 30 DAYS?

I realize this question may cause you to wonder if I have a firm grasp on reality. However, just for a second, suppose your spouse looked at you and said, "Let's travel the world for a month!" If you were like most business owners, you would laugh because you know you would be totally out of business if you did not work for 30 days. Time and time again, I meet with business owners who have built owner-based business systems that only work if the owner works long hours. These business owners lack time freedom, financial freedom, and an exit strategy for the business. - Clay Clark

NOTABLE QUOTABLE

"IF YOU ARE WILLING TO DO ONLY WHAT IS EASY, LIFE WILL BE HARD. BUT IF YOU ARE WILLING TO DO WHAT IS HARD, LIFE WILL BE EASY."

T. Harv Eker

(*New York Times* best-selling author of *Secrets of the Millionaire Mind*)

However, these same doctors and medical professionals state that they started their practices to achieve both financial and time freedom while helping their patients to get well. At the end of the day, if the success of your practice is judged based upon whether it has achieved its purpose to create the time and financial freedom that you desire, it should be considered a failure if it does not do that. As Alex's mentor tells him in the fantastic book "The Goal" by Eliyahu Goldratt, "a business should serve a purpose, and its performance should be measured against this purpose."

Now, if you were playing third grade soccer, I am sure a socialist referee would give you a 2nd place trophy and some ice cream to keep you from considering the profundity of the fact that your practice is currently failing you. But this is not third grade soccer, and as of the writing of this book, medicine has not yet been fully consumed by the socialist hordes. This is your livelihood. And it is time to face reality.

How long would your business and practice last if you were on vacation for a month, or were abducted by aliens for 30 days?

-Dr. Timothy Johnson

3.3

DO NOT FEEL BAD, BUT DO NOT GET STUCK

I started my first business in my college dorm room and I have launched over a dozen successful ventures.

Every time I have personally launched a successful or have helped to coach a successful business, it has started with a relentless tenacious and ridiculously motivated individual who is willing to scratch and claw their way to profitability. However, once you begin to figure out what works, you must have the knowledge, discipline, and focus needed to document your workflow, operational systems, and turnkey marketing moves. Otherwise, you will be trapped inside of your own profitable practice. - Clay Clark

---

NOTABLE QUOTABLE

"MOST PEOPLE ARE SITTING ON THEIR OWN DIAMOND MINES. THE SUREST WAYS TO LOSE YOUR DIAMOND MINE ARE TO GET BORED, BECOME OVERAMBITIOUS, OR START THINKING THAT THE GRASS IS GREENER ON THE OTHER SIDE. FIND YOUR CORE FOCUS, STICK TO IT, AND DEVOTE YOUR TIME AND RESOURCES TO EXCELLING AT IT."

Gino Wickman

(The bestselling author of the book
Traction: Get a Grip on Your Business)

"THE DIFFERENCE BETWEEN GREAT PEOPLE AND EVERYONE ELSE IS THAT GREAT PEOPLE CREATE THEIR LIVES ACTIVELY, WHILE EVERYONE ELSE IS CREATED BY THEIR LIVES, PASSIVELY WAITING TO SEE WHERE LIFE TAKES THEM NEXT. THE DIFFERENCE BETWEEN THE TWO IS LIVING FULLY AND JUST EXISTING."

Michael Gerber

(Bestselling author of the *E-Myth* book series)

3.4

BUILD YOUR PRACTICE WITH
THE END IN MIND

I GUARANTEE THAT YOU WILL ACHIEVE SUCCESS IF YOU FOLLOW THE PRACTICAL STEPS OUTLINED IN THIS BOOK. However, you must have your vision for your life fully cemented into your mind at all times as you are building your business. My friend, I love my life because I know what I want and I know what I am about all day, every day. I know what I call my "F6 Goals." My F6 goals are the goals I have for my faith, family, finances, fitness, friendship, and fun.

-Clay Clark

NOTABLE QUOTABLE

"DRIFTING, WITHOUT AIM OR PURPOSE, IS THE FIRST CAUSE OF FAILURE."

- Napoleon Hill

(Bestselling author of
Think and Grow Rich and *Outwitting the Devil*)

You must intentionally know and take the time to clearly write down your F6 Goals because you will certainly never "drift" toward the achievement of them.

\- Dr. Timothy Johnson

I am a husband and father with five kids, 24 chickens and 13 cats; and I prefer spending time alone with my family, listening to R&B music, attending strong R&B concerts, engaging only in mutually beneficial friendships, watching TD Jakes sermons online, watching all Patriots football games, and chasing my wife around whenever possible (that is how you create five kids, you see). My friend, if you are going to go through the HELL of starting a business, you must build a thriving business model and medical practice that is not dependent upon you. So I am going to challenge you here for a moment. Take the assessment. What are your F6 Goals? \- Clay Clark

Define your F6 Goals (Faith, Family, Finances, Fitness, Friendships, and Fun) right now!

Faith _____

Family _____

Finance _____

Fitness _____

Friendship _____

Fun _____

- Clay Clark

3.5

DR. TIM'S PRESCRIPTION FOR SUCCESS:
WORKING HARDER AND SMARTER

I have played the same game you are playing. I sacrificed and cried and questioned my maker through years of organic chemistry, pointless biology classes, and memorizing the Krebs Cycle. I know the blood, sweat, and tears you have to put into getting to where you are. And part of what got you here was keeping your head down, ignoring that stress and desire to have a life, and the frustration of delaying gratification. Nobody knows how to work harder than a doctor who has completed medical school and residency.

But as author and executive coach Marshall Goldsmith would say, "what got you here will not get you there." The good news is you ARE almost there.

Most doctors suffer from the misconception that after finishing their medical training, they are complete. This belief is true if you just want to be an employee, a doctor who works for a living, albeit a good living. But if you want to take it to the next level, you have to realize that your medical training was just your ticket to the show. Now that you are through the door, you have to take it to the next level.

Think of your business like rounding on patients in the hospital. It is just you. You have to see every patient, check every lab and vital sign, write every note. You cannot see many patients alone, can you? So you hire some interns to do all the work you hate doing. It is nice that you do not have to change catheters or spend hours on the phone. But, these interns do not know a lot.

It is almost more work at first finding the interns and teaching them everything, keeping an eye on them. So you hire some former interns who can help manage the interns. Now the chief resident manages the team of interns, while you do whatever it is attendees do while the residents work.

The point is that your practice is here to serve you, to give you time and financial freedom. We're going to speak at detailed length about the systems, checklists, workflows, and processes needed to scale your medical practice. However, it is important that you understand an important principle up front: working harder and working smarter are not mutually exclusive ideas. It is not binary. It is not one or the other.

As a business owner, I encourage you to build checklists, scripts, and systems for everything to save you both time and money , but that is not to say that you will immediately begin working less. Growing a business is a grind, and you will put in more hours doing it than anything you have done before. In order to build time freedom-creating practice, you will likely have to work MORE than what you are currently working now to create all the systems, but it is worth it.

-Clay Clark

This book has been written to help you navigate through how to work SMARTER, and you are in TOTAL CONTROL of the working HARDER part. The questions you must ask yourself are, "Where is my destination?, What are my goals?, And What is my why?" And then, "How much profit do I need to generate annually to get there?" Your work ethic should mirror your overall sense of urgency and willingness to get there.

-Dr. Timothy Johnson

"AN ORGANIZATION'S CAPABILITIES RESIDE IN TWO PLACES. THE FIRST IS IN ITS PROCESSES— THE METHODS BY WHICH PEOPLE HAVE LEARNED TO TRANSFORM INPUTS OF LABOR, ENERGY, MATERIALS, INFORMATION, CASH, AND TECHNOLOGY INTO OUTPUTS OF HIGHER VALUE. THE SECOND IS IN THE ORGANIZATION'S VALUES, WHICH ARE THE CRITERIA THAT MANAGERS AND EMPLOYEES IN THE ORGANIZATION USE WHEN MAKING PRIORITIZATION DECISIONS."

Clayton Christensen

(The legendary Harvard Business school professor and former ThrivetimeShow.com guest)

Years ago I had the pleasure of working with a clinic for men suffering from low testosterone. The doctor was a quality dude working 70 hours per week, every week. EVERY WEEK!!! He had seen spikes in his business from time to time over the years as they hired my team to help him with his marketing. However, as his revenue grew so did his workload. Why? He had never documented their inbound phone call scripts or any of the process that he personally used when seeing patients. He had no customer relationship management (CRM) software in place and no checklists for how and when to clean his bathrooms.

However, after 60 days working 1 to 2 hours per week on the business he was able to get his life back by simply investing the time needed to create the systems needed for other less skilled people to perform the tasks. - Clay Clark

---

NOTABLE QUOTABLE

"YOU DO NOT GET PAID FOR THE HOUR. YOU GET PAID FOR THE VALUE YOU BRING TO THE HOUR."

Jim Rohn

(Best-selling author and world-renowned motivational speaker)

When you take the time needed to create systems you must also invest the time needed to make sure that your team is actually following the systems. Your team must know that their calls are being recorded for quality assurance and they must know that their paychecks are tied to their performance and overall conversion rates. Your team must know how and when they need to execute their daily marketing tasks and when those bathrooms need to be cleaned. - Dr. Timothy johnson

---

Just 12 months after this particular doctor implemented these systems he was able to grow his medical practice by nearly 400% and was able to reduce the hours spent working in the clinic to just 35 hours per week (down from 70 hours per week). Today his business is bigger AND less time consuming. After hiring another doctor, he now spends about one hour per day to follow-up and verify that all of the daily checklists are being completed. - Clay Clark

You should strive to build a medical practice so solid it does not actually need you. When you reach the point when you can spend your entire day away from the business and no one texts you, calls you, or e-mails you for help, you will know that you have made it. To create this time freedom, you must create tight systems and business processes. However, the hardest part of stream-lining and working on your business is realizing that this might be the first time in your career when just working harder will not produce the systematic solutions you need to create both the time and financial freedom you seek. In fact, your intense work ethic may actually be part of the problem when working on creating time-saving, efficient processes.

Medical school is hard, but it is not complex. For example, the first two years of medical school are nothing more than thousands of facts. During these two years you have some tests, then at the end of those two years you have a big test. It is not complex, just really hard. People who win at medical school do so because they keep their head down, they shut up, and they do the work. Well, business is not like that.

- Dr. Timothy Johnson

Quit working hard and start working smart. Start thinking, "How can I make a system to fix this problem so I never have to deal with it again?"

Before we start, we need to figure out where you currently are. Take a moment to rate your organization's overall competency and efficiency on a scale of 1 to 10 (with 10 being the highest) in the following areas:

1. Branding
2. Marketing
3. Sales
4. Service Quality
5. Collections
6. Accounting
7. Human Resources
8. Scalability
9. Profitability
10. Management
11. Public Relations

- Clay Clark

NOTABLE QUOTABLE

"NATURE CANNOT BE TRICKED OR CHEATED. SHE WILL GIVE UP TO YOU THE OBJECT OF YOUR STRUGGLES ONLY AFTER YOU HAVE PAID HER PRICE."

- Napoleon Hill

(Best-selling author of *Think & Grow Rich*)3.6

FORESEEABLE MILESTONES

Nearly every medical practice follows a predictable pathway. The practice first struggles to survive and to make a profit and to stand out in the clutter of commerce. The founding doctor consumes every possible form of energy drink known to man while attempting to become the world's best marketer, accountant, manager, and public relations wizard. If the founder keeps their sanity while creating enough profit to sustain the practice, the owner then begins to build a successful practice totally dependent on him. No systems are in place, but the profitability is consistent and so the owner relaxes because he has finally started to develop some traction despite the doubters who said it could not be done.

Eventually the owner realizes that one day they would like to leave the office for 30 minutes per week to enjoy a burrito or to some day enjoy the foreign concept known as "taking a vacation." Once the owner COMMITS TO SYSTEMATIZING THE PRACTICE IN A DUPLICABLE WAY THAT ALLOWS THEM TO CONSISTENTLY CREATE A SUSTAINABLE PROFIT BY ADDING VALUE TO THEIR IDEAL AND LIKELY PATIENTS, great things start happening.

once the practice has turn-key traction-producing systems in place that practice can produce profits while they are on vacation with their family or in the backyard attempting to find their five-year-old daughter's shoe (which I currently spend half of my life doing. With five kids, I am very aware that the stores sell kid's shoes in pairs, yet my kids are always just losing one. I basically needed to achieve both financial and time freedom just so that I would have enough time to find shoes and buy shoes when I cannot find them). My friend, I want to ask you: Why do you want to build and grow a successful practice?

Imagine truly having both the time freedom and financial freedom necessary for complete flexibility in your schedule, with total control over your calendar. What activities would you spend your time doing?

Monday _____

Tuesday _____

Wednesday _____

Thursday _____

Friday _____

Saturday _____

Sunday _____

- Clay Clark

NOTABLE QUOTABLE

"OUR GOALS CAN ONLY BE REACHED THROUGH THE
VEHICLE OF A PLAN, IN WHICH WE MUST FERVENTLY
BELIEVE, AND UPON WHICH WE MUST VIGOROUSLY
ACT. THERE IS NO OTHER ROUTE TO SUCCESS."

Pablo Picasso

(Renowned painter, sculptor, ceramicist,
stage designer, and playwright)

4.0

THE PRACTICAL STEPS OF TURNING YOUR DREAMS INTO REALITY

Alright, now I need your permission to GET INTENSE HERE FOR A SECOND and I need for you to UNDERLINE AND HIGHLIGHT THE FOLLOWING WORDS. Nobody cares about your success more than you and in most cases, even at all. I care and you care, and potentially you have a spouse, partner, or friend who really cares, but NOBODY IS GOING TO CARE ABOUT YOUR PRACTICE MORE THAN YOU.

- Dr. Timothy Johnson

"DISCIPLINE IS THE BRIDGE BETWEEN GOALS AND
ACCOMPLISHMENT."

Jim Rohn

(Best-selling author and world-famous motivational speaker)

When it is time for your first all-nighter, most people are not going to be with you cheering and helping you along. My friend, if you are going to go down this path of turning your dreams into reality, I know the way and the super-successful guests that I interview daily on my Thrivetime Show podcast know the way too. We are here with this book, our two-day workshops, our podcast, and our one-on-one coaching. But you must not allow yourself to get stuck. Give us a call if you ever get stuck, but you must keep moving. Visit ThrivetimeShow.com to schedule a one-on-one 13 point assessment with me personally. You must COMMIT TO TAKING MASSIVE ACTION. My friend, here is the process that you must go through.

4.1

STAGE 1: GIVING BIRTH

You need to formalize your business plan, raise capital, create your logo and website, create your initial marketing materials, and see if the world will pay you for your solutions. During this phase you are going to work countless hours as you try to encourage yourself, fight off doubters, and tell your inner "I am-scared-out-of-my-mind-that-I am-an-idiot-if-this-fails" to shut up. - Dr. Timothy Johnson

4.1.2

DR. TIM'S PRESCRIPTION
FOR SUCCESS: IGNORE THE DOUBTERS,
ESPECIALLY YOURSELF

We all have that guy inside us. He tells us we are not good enough. He wonders whether we have the right stuff. Want to hear a secret nobody talks about? Most people think like this. Most people have that guy inside him. Think of the biggest guy in your industry. If you are a cardiologist, think Michael Debakey. If you are in ophthalmology, think Charles Kelman. If you are a neurosurgeon, think Ben Carson.

I guarantee they all doubted themselves every step of the way. What is the difference between them and everyone else? They did not pay attention to this little doubting voice. My friend, you cannot let emotions get in the way of the motions you need to take to achieve your goals in life.

If you are crazy enough to go out there and start a practice, this will be your life for a while. However, with our help, you can get through this phase much more quickly. - Dr. Timothy Johnson

NOTABLE QUOTABLE

"HERE'S TO THE CRAZY ONES, THE MISFITS, THE REBELS, THE TROUBLEMAKERS, THE ROUND PEGS IN THE SQUARE HOLES... THE ONES WHO SEE THINGS DIFFERENTLY -- THEY'RE NOT FOND OF RULES... YOU CAN QUOTE THEM, DISAGREE WITH THEM, GLORIFY OR VILIFY THEM, BUT THE ONLY THING YOU CANNOT DO IS IGNORE THEM BECAUSE THEY CHANGE THINGS... THEY PUSH THE HUMAN RACE FORWARD, AND WHILE SOME MAY SEE THEM AS THE CRAZY ONES, WE SEE GENIUS, BECAUSE THE ONES WHO ARE CRAZY ENOUGH TO THINK THAT THEY CAN CHANGE THE WORLD, ARE THE ONES WHO DO."

Steve Jobs

(Co-founder of Apple, former CEO of Pixar, and the founder of NeXT)

4.1.3

IT IS ABOUT TIME TO FORM THAT LIMITED LIABILITY COMPANY

As a medical professional, you will want to form an LLC to ensure that you do not lose everything you have personally saved up when you get sued, and you will eventually get sued. To simplify and demystify the process for you (because people tend to fear what they do not know), here are the steps necessary to form an LLC.

- Dr. Timothy Johnson

Fun Fact:

"90% of all businesses are engaged in litigation at any given time."
Forbes

"You are going to get sued, here's how not to get screwed"
https://www.forbes.com/sites/basharubin/2014/07/14/youre-going-to-get-sued/#387d8d937f08

1. Accept emotionally that you will get sued at some point (which is the main reason you need to form an LLC in the first place).

2. Find an attorney to help you form an LLC. Attempting to form an LLC by yourself is dumb and will negate the entire purpose of forming an LLC when you discover that your LLC cannot protect you because it was filed incorrectly. Once you are sued, it is too late! I recommend without reservation using the law firm I use, WintersKing.com

3. Select the business name for your LLC.

4. Hire an attorney to write your articles of incorporation.

5. Hire an attorney to create an operating agreement.

6. Hire an attorney to publish a notice in the states that require it.

7. Hire an attorney to get the appropriate licenses and permits.

- Clay Clark

This just in! "I highly recommend that you hire WintersKing.com. They have represented me for years and their current and former clients include: Pastor TD Jakes, Pastor Joel Osteen, Pastor Joyce Meyer, Pastor Craig Groeschel, and more." - Clay Clark

4.1.4

DR. TIM'S PRESCRIPTION FOR SUCCESS:
BUSINESS PLAN NOW?

Real Quick – There is a common business misconception that you need a business plan to even begin an entrepreneurial journey. I mean, who would start a trip without a detailed map? WRONG. That is not really how the world works. Think of it like walking in to see an Emergency Department patient with chest pain. Sure you are thinking of five deadly causes of chest pain. But you would not start treatment for a pulmonary embolism or relieve a tension pneumothorax without first gathering data and touching base with reality. You would talk to the patient and examine him first. Let observations and reality guide your next step. The same thing is true for business. It would be foolish to spend copious amounts of time developing a world-class business plan and pitch deck if you are going to pivot at least 934 times after you have created that initial plan. - Dr. Timothy Johnson

---

NOTABLE QUOTABLE

"THE DOERS ARE THE MAJOR THINKERS. THE PEOPLE
THAT REALLY CREATE THE THINGS THAT CHANGE
THIS INDUSTRY ARE BOTH THE THINKER AND DOER IN
ONE PERSON."

Steve Jobs

(Co-founder of Apple, the founder of
NeXT and the former CEO of Pixar)

4.2

STAGE 2

Raising a Baby Business - At this point, you want to make sure you do not drop the ball and ensure that you deliver a consistent and quality experience to your ideal and likely buyers and patients. At this point, you spend most of your time in this stage scrambling around answering the phone, training your cousin to take payments from customers, trying to convince your mom to answer the phone, and hoping that the minivan you drive to work does not explode after it passes 200,000 miles on the odometer. You are irritated that your first non-family employee broke an instrument you cannot afford to replace because, oh by the way, you owe a quarter million dollars in student loan debt. - Dr. Timothy Johnson

Fun Fact:

"There are over 44 MILLION student debtors (in the United States) and researchers estimate that as many as 40% could default... but canceling the student loan debt does not make the problem disappear."

Kevin Carey: https://www.nytimes.com/2019/06/25/upshot/student-loan-debt-forgiveness.html

During this time of chaotic commerce, you must also formulate your inbound and outbound phone scripts. You must document the steps you have to take to deliver an outstanding level of patient care.

You must create an employee handbook, organize your files, and develop a naming system for your computer files that makes sense. You are trying to get all of this done while taking your kids to soccer practice and figuring out what kind of checklist you need to get your public bathroom to stop smelling like the rotting remains of a road kill animal. During this time in your business, you must figure out what works and what does not and make the time needed to transform your findings into checklists, systems, repeatable processes, scripts and templates that other humans can actually use - Clay Clark

4.3

STAGE 3

The Bipolar Teenager - If you have ever raised a teenager, been around a teenager, or were a teenager, then you will know what I am talking about. It is during this time that you are just trying to get everybody to CALM DOWN AND STOP LOSING THEIR FREAKING MINDS!!! Just like teenagers, overloaded with hormones and freaking out about their bodies that are changing so rapidly they do not even recognize themselves in the mirror, when you get to this point in your business you are going to be acting a little nuts by default. One moment you are PUMPED and you KNOW THAT THIS WILL BE THE BEST YEAR EVER. The next moment THE ENTIRE UNIVERSE HATES YOU AND YOU ARE NEVER GOING TO GET OVER THAT COLD. Exhausted, you press on because you financially cannot afford to stop now. - Dr. Timothy Johnson

You are tired of being tired and you are irritated when your team members tell you how tired they are after an 8-hour shift, BECAUSE YOU HAVE BEEN UP SINCE TWO IN THE MORNING AND YOU HAVEN'T TAKEN A FREAKING DAY OFF IN FOUR YEARS. Because you are so emotional at this point, I am encouraging you to mellow out and begin to F.O.C.U.S. (Focus On Core tasks Until Success) on creating six systems as soon as possible.

System 1 – Define Your Three-Legged Marketing Stool - You must figure out the three most profitable ways to reach your ideal and likely patients and buyers.

System 2 – Learn to Dominate Internet Marketing - Sometimes I hate to be the guy who has to point this out to doctors, attorneys, bakers, dentists, neurologists, roofers, real estate agents, hair stylists, carpet cleaners, appliance sellers, retailers, and everybody else... THE INTERNET IS STARTING TO CATCH ON. In all sincerity, people use their smartphone for everything so you are just being dumb if you do not know what you are doing on the Internet when it comes to building your website, social media marketing, targeting your ideal and likely buyers, and closing deals.

System 3 – The ABC Sales Machine – You must define specifically how your ABC (Always Be Closing) Sales Machine works if you are not the one personally taking payments from your patients.

System 4 - Define Your Product and Service Delivery Systems - You must refine and document your systems to the point that an honest moron could deliver your quality services to your patients

System 5 - Accounting Systems - You must invest the time needed to define your break-even point, your profit per patient, your lifetime patient value, when your taxes are due, and what the heck is going on with your numbers. If you fail to do this, you will lose.

System 6 - Hiring, Managing, and Training People - As long as your practice is based on Planet Earth, you are going to have to manage people. Finding, inspiring, training, and holding people accountable has proven to be almost impossible without following the time-tested best-practice hiring and management systems found in this book. Good news. We will teach you how to do this. - Clay Clark

---

NOTABLE QUOTABLE

"THE ABILITY TO DEAL WITH PEOPLE IS AS PURCHASABLE A COMMODITY AS SUGAR OR COFFEE AND I WILL PAY MORE FOR THAT ABILITY THAN FOR ANY OTHER UNDER THE SUN."

John D. Rockefeller

(The world's richest man during his lifetime who had to drop out of school at the age of 16 to support his mother financially)

"I TRY TO BUY STOCK IN BUSINESSES THAT ARE SO WONDERFUL THAT AN IDIOT CAN RUN THEM BECAUSE SOONER OR LATER, ONE WILL."

Warren Buffett

(One the of the most prolific and
successful investors of all time)

My friend, these six systems comprise the foundation of every successful medical business, so you must learn how to master these six systems. Once you master them, you will be like the Yoda of business (except I hope you do not choose to live alone in a swamp after achieving your success). For a deep dive into these six systems, check out our foundational book written by the co-author of this book, Clay Clark, *Start Here: The world's best business growth and consulting book.*

- Dr. Timothy Johnson

4.4

STAGE 4

The Young Adult - As an adult, you and I know that we are "supposed to act like adults" and generally we do, but occasionally we lose our minds. MOST ENTREPRENEURS GET STUCK HERE BECAUSE THEY ARE THE ONES WHO RUN EVERY ASPECT

OF THE DAILY BUSINESS OPERATIONS, THEY DRUM UP ALL
OF THE HUGE SALES DEALS, AND THEY MUST MAKE EVERY
KEY DECISION. You must learn to train people and you must learn
how to grow your team into the mature adults you need them to be.

- Clay Clark

4.5

STAGE 5

The Mature Adult - The goal at this stage of your practice
development is to be wise and to be viewed as a source of wisdom for
your team, whom you keep busy executing your repeatable processes
and systems. At this phase in the business game, your focus needs to be
on delegating and growing your people. *- Dr. Timothy Johnson*

4.6

STAGE 6

The Bruce Wayne - Once you have successfully trained your staff
how to train people and have installed all of the systems needed for
your business to run effectively and efficiently without you, it is time
for you to focus on incrementally improving your practices, processes,
and systems. Strategically coach up your leaders to take your practice
to the next level.

You need to be working on your business and not in your practice at this point so you can focus on other more important things like "running the city."

This is the stage of business that business superheroes reach. I once spent the majority of an afternoon with my business partner and *Thrivetime Show* podcast host, CEO, Doctor Robert Zoellner as he attempted to bring balance to his fish aquarium. He had recently acquired an exotic fish (the only one of its kind in Oklahoma) and the other fish inside the fish tank were trying to eat it. Dr. Zoellner spent hours researching what could be done to bring balance back to his aquatic ecosystem. It was incredible. What business owner has this kind of time? Wouldn't it be nice to be able to spend your day trying to solve the problems inside your aquarium rather than trying to find the quarters that may have fallen behind your car's seats so that you make payroll this week and so that you can afford to keep your practice going?

Have you ever noticed how few hours Bruce Wayne seems to be working? Now I have never spent any time with Batman, but it seems as though Wayne Enterprises is doing pretty well without Bruce actually processing each individual transaction or answering every phone call.

- Clay Clark

4.7

STAGE 7

The Elon Musk - At this stage of the business, you should start to view your team members truly as partners and your goal is to constantly make sure that your top people are focused on their highest and best use at all times. By now, you should have coached your people up to be the leaders needed to help your practice to dominate the marketplace. Your team should all work in concert with you to help you refine, build, and create the duplicable business systems that you are going to need to truly scale your business.

- Dr. Timothy Johnson

4.8

STAGE 8

Drop the Mic - In my first business (in my former life as the founder of www.DJConnection.com), I worked as an entertainer. I wanted to take each event to the next level and the audience to leave stunned and wanting more because we had just taken them to a place they have never gone before. When you have rocked a show or speaking event at this level, you "drop the mic" with nothing left to say. You have dominated. Everyone is cheering. Then you walk off stage. As an entertainer I have had the pleasure of doing this dozens of times, and as an entrepreneur I have been able to do this a few times as well.

You know that you have arrived and that your business has reached the "Drop the Mic" level once your business is:

Dependent on processes and systems and not people.

Stable with a competitive and goal-achieving leadership team in place.

Secure with powerful "guardrails" or controls in place that keep your team accountable on a daily basis for taking the action steps required to produce predictable success.

Flush with patients who come to your practice for the products and services they want and not to you specifically see you as the owner.

Once you have taken your business to this level, it is now the appropriate time to consider an exit strategy. My friend, this does not necessarily mean selling the practice. It just means you are no longer personally required to GRIND INTENSELY FOR THE BUSINESS TO THRIVE. At this level you can choose to be actively involved in the business or not because you have considered six main exit strategies:

1. You can exponentially grow the medical business into different territories, states, or countries. Example: I have helped many clients do this(including DelrichtResearch.com, and BodyCentral.com). They know how to deliver care so we refined their marketing systems, lead conversion systems, accounting systems, and quality control systems which allowed them to open up multiple locations.

2. You can own the business passively while only being involved in the daily operations and strategic decisions for four hours per week or less.

Example: I employ this strategy with several of my businesses. I have put in the hard work and now I simply follow up at certain scheduled hours each week to confirm things are running properly.

3. You could sell the business if you wanted to. Example: The DJConnection.com systems worked and worked well. People knew the systems worked and constantly approached me to sell the business to them. Eventually, I agreed. I did the same thing with Party Perfect, a company I systemized and sold to PartyProRents.com. On a smaller level, I also did this with the professional video production company I started, Cherished Traditions Videography, EpicPhotos.com, etc.

4. You can franchise a turnkey business model. Example: I have had the pleasure to coach and work with Jonathan Barnett at Oxi Fresh Carpet Cleaning (www.OxiFresh.com). He has literally now opened up over 400 + locations and is also a partner in the Elephant in the Room Men's Grooming Lounge (www.EITRLounge.com). He now has three corporate-owned locations in Tulsa, OK and two franchise locations in Oklahoma City, OK.

5. You have the option to license the business. Example: Many companies know that their brand recognition is so powerful that others will pay millions just to license their brands. Think about the New England Patriots or the Alabama Crimson Tide. Companies pay

millions to put the Patriot or Alabama logo on merchandise like hats, cups, t-shirts, and more. Another company, Luxottica pays millions to put the Nike, Eddie Bauer, or Gucci brand name on prescription glasses.

6. You could bring on investors through outside venture capital or private equity and take the business all over the world quickly with millions to invest in scaling your proven strategies and systems. Example: Elizabeth Cutler and Julie Rice who started SoulCycle sought to revolutionize the fitness industry. They built a business model that worked and that people love. Wealthy investors, including the quasi-famous billionaire and real estate guru Stephen M. Ross and his company Related, own the health club chain Equinox and acquired a majority share of SoulCycle in 2011.

- Clay Clark

4.9

CHECKING IN TO MAKE SURE THAT YOU ARE
LEARNING SOMETHING...

Now that we have discussed all eight stages of a successful business' development, it is important that you take a moment to "marinate," as Paul Pressey would say (Paul Pressey is my friend and a former coach of the Orlando Magic, Golden State Warriors, San Antonio Spurs, Boston Celtics, and Los Angeles Lakers). Right now, get out a pen and put a checkbox by which one of the following statements best describes you so that you can know which level of business development you and your business are at today.

☐ Stage 1 - You are super excited about your new idea, but you are still trying to raise the capital, refine that business plan, and you are getting ready to start that new business.

☐ Stage 2 - You are trying to show the world that you are not crazy by just making your practice profitable. You are hustling to bring in new patients and to deliver the high quality of care your patients deserve. You do not sleep much, but you are excited, like when you are in love for the first time and you keep meeting your girlfriend for 3-hour make out sessions behind the Learning Resources Center at Oral Roberts University. (I am sorry I just got super personal there. I will make sure that does not happen again until the next page)

☐ Stage 3 - Your business model is actually quasi-sustainable. You are able to consistently bring in new patients and deliver on what you promise, but it is draining. At this point, you are your patient's top doctor, salesperson, service / product provider, and accountant. At the end of the day, the company begins and ends with you.

☐ Stage 4 - Your medical business is doing well and you are gaining traction and new business quickly, but you have not yet developed any other leaders or top-level managers. You realize that you need quality people to turn your big vision into reality and you have recently realized that you need to become a developer of people if you are ever going to develop your idea and take it to the NEXT LEVEL. You are spending massive amounts of time per week attempting to improve both your business processes, your leadership, and your management team.

☐ Stage 5 - Your team views you as a source of wisdom, your business is absolutely beginning to produce big revenues and you are excited about it. You have now developed at least three leaders and managers who are capable of running the daily operations of your business.

☐ Stage 6 - You no longer must work in the daily operations of your business, and you are beginning to make large amounts of money while no longer exchanging your time for money. You could spend massive amounts of time pursuing your non-business-related hobbies and passions, but you desire to take your business to the next level.

☐ Stage 7 - You have developed a team of hard-working strategic leaders and are confident they could do your job as well as you, if not better. You are comfortable financially, but you see the vision of your company expanding regionally, nationally, and even internationally.

☐ Stage 8 - Your business model is now so well-refined that it may make sense to license the business, franchise the business, sell the business, or bring in an infusion of venture capital and private equity. You want to positively impact the world and now you are looking for a way to scale your vision.

- Clay Clark

4.10

DR. TIM'S PRESCRIPTION FOR SUCCESS:
HONEST EVALUATIONS

Throughout the book, we will ask you to evaluate yourself to get you thinking about your current reality. For most medical professionals, this is the first time you have been asked and GIVEN PERMISSION to be candid about your practice. You will not help yourself by artificially scoring yourself above your current reality. Remember, this book is about YOUR business and moving beyond just working in it. Use this as an opportunity to create an honest baseline to improve upon and understand that we are going to help you through every stage of this process. Your success in your business is our sincere passion.

- Dr. Timothy Johnson

NOTABLE QUOTABLE

"FACE REALITY AS IT IS, NOT AS IT WAS OR AS YOU WISH IT TO BE."

Jack Welch

(Former CEO of General Electric who grew the company over 4,000% during his tenure)

"MOST ENTREPRENEURS ARE MERELY TECHNICIANS WITH AN
ENTREPRENEURIAL SEIZURE. MOST ENTREPRENEURS FAIL BECAUSE THEY ARE
WORKING IN THEIR BUSINESS RATHER THAN ON THEIR BUSINESS."
- MICHAEL GERBER
AUTHOR OF 'THE E-MYTH REVISITED'

Once you have invested the time and money into building world-class business systems they will not work unless you take the 5 following action steps:

1. Trust but verify everything and everybody
2. Always create a followup loop
3. Hire consistant Mystery Shoppers
4. Create a pipeline of inbound new people
5. Fire when ready

MAKE IT DUPLICATABLE

Phase #2

5.1

CREATE A BUSINESS BASED UPON THE FOUNDATIONS OF A DUPLICABLE PROCESS, A WINNING TEAM, AND WELL-DEFINED GUARDRAILS

If you had millions of dollars to invest and SHOCKINGLY, your goal was to make a good return on your investment, which would you rather invest in:

- A stable, scalable, and profitable medical practice

- A practice entirely dependent on one person, where no systems are recorded and every decision must go through one person

I have worked with many doctors and dentists over the years. I can tell you from first-hand experience that most medical professionals build systems dependent on key people who are the only ones who know the passwords, who have all of the skills, and who could actually kill the company simply by deciding to take another job somewhere else. This is not a good thing.

My friend, when you build a business based on documented processes, checklists, and systems you eliminate the necessity of hiring geniuses. When you implement sound systems, you can focus on hiring honest and diligent people. These systems allows you to hire for character and not for skill.

This is where you want to be. When you decide to build your business upon processes, checklists, controls and systems, you make it much easier to find key employees to fill key positions and makes it DRAMATICALLY EASIER to grow your practice exponentially.

Want to hear a secret? Most employees deep down crave structure and systems in place to guide them. By diligently working to install the systems, checklists, and processes for each position within your company, you will make it EXPONENTIALLY EASIER to hire new people. If you would like to see an example of best-practice checklists, systems, and processes, email us at info@thrivetimeshow.com and we will send you examples.

- Clay Clark

5.2

WHAT THE HECK IS A SYSTEM?
SYSTEMS ARE REALLY THE SKELETON OF ANY
SUCCESSFUL BUSINESS

A system is a step-by-step process or checklist that has been created to dependably produce predictable and satisfactory results. A system should be quickly accessible to your team members who need to use these systems on a daily basis to minimize errors and avoid providing patient care and customer service that is less than ideal.

- Dr. Timothy Johnson

"CHECKLISTS SEEM ABLE TO DEFEND ANYONE, EVEN THE EXPERIENCED, AGAINST FAILURE IN MANY MORE TASKS THAN WE REALIZED."

Atul Gawande

(Atul Gawande, MD, MPH is the CEO of Haven, the Amazon, Berkshire Hathaway, SP Morgan, Chase Health, and the globally recognized surgeon, writer, and public health leader.)

When referencing checklists, I am talking about a specific list of items that your company will use to hold your team accountable for delivering servicing and care to each and every one of your patients. These lists need to cover nearly every aspect of your business, from the smallest tasks to the most complex. These checklists need to cover the processes that you will use to greet and sign in patients to clean bathrooms, train your staff, to onboard employees, manage the finances, and beyond. If you expect anyone on your team to do anything on a consistent and repeatable basis, you must create a checklist for this.

 - Clay Clark

"(WITHOUT A CHECKLIST) THE VOLUME AND COMPLEXITY OF WHAT WE KNOW HAS EXCEEDED OUR INDIVIDUAL ABILITY TO DELIVER ITS BENEFITS CORRECTLY, SAFELY, OR RELIABLY. KNOWLEDGE HAS BOTH SAVED US AND BURDENED US."

Atul Gawande

(The bestselling author of *The Checklist Manifesto*, a surgeon and a professor in the Department of Health Policy and Management at the Harvard T.H. Chan School of Public Health)

Once upon a time, I was explaining to my very successful uncle how it was impossible to teach adult men without entertainment and disk jockey experience how to become successful disc jockeys. He then explained to me that if I believed that, then my company would never grow. He said it is entirely possible to duplicate nearly any process if you are detailed and committed to training. Seven years after that conversation, I had built such a repeatable system for DJing that I am 100% confident that I could teach you or anyone with a coachable spirit how to act as a professional emcee and disc jockey with 15 hours or less of hands-on training. - Clay Clark

---

NOTABLE QUOTABLE

"WHETHER YOU THINK YOU CAN, OR THINK YOU CANNOT – YOU ARE RIGHT."

Henry Ford

(The self-made millionaire and founder
of the Ford Motor Company)

As you begin to introduce these systems to your team, you must know your team will initially push back and fight against the idea of systemizing every aspect of their job. They will start to worry that they can now be "easily replaced" as a result of these systems. However, you must point out to them that great business systems are not in place to allow for the replacement of people. They are in place to enable your team to consistently wow clients and even allow members of your team to occasionally take a day off without a nuclear meltdown occurring in your medical practice. Imagine that! - Clay Clark

---

NOTABLE QUOTABLE

"WE DO NOT LIKE CHECKLISTS. THEY CAN BE PAINSTAKING. THEY'RE NOT MUCH FUN. BUT I DO NOT THINK THE ISSUE HERE IS MERE LAZINESS. THERE'S SOMETHING DEEPER, MORE VISCERAL GOING ON WHEN PEOPLE WALK AWAY NOT ONLY FROM SAVING LIVES, BUT FROM MAKING MONEY. IT SOMEHOW FEELS BENEATH US TO USE A CHECKLIST, AN EMBARRASSMENT. IT RUNS COUNTER TO DEEPLY HELD BELIEFS ABOUT HOW THE TRULY GREAT AMONG US—THOSE WE ASPIRE TO BE—HANDLE SITUATIONS OF HIGH STAKES AND COMPLEXITY. THE TRULY GREAT ARE DARING. THEY IMPROVISE. THEY DO NOT HAVE PROTOCOLS AND CHECKLISTS. MAYBE OUR IDEA OF HEROISM NEEDS UPDATING."

Atul Gawande

(The bestselling author of *The Checklist Manifesto*, a surgeon and a professor of surgery at Harvard Medical School)

Dr. Tim's Prescription for Success: Moving from Working IN Your Practice to Working ON It.

This section may have the biggest impact on a medical professional who simply feels like they lack progress in growing their practice despite the fact that they are working so hard at operating it. But it is one that most people resist because they feel it might be stifling or too robotic, and their employees do not need or want it. But think of protocols in medicine. Sure we could allow human creativity to thrive and let doctors and nurses come up with the treatment solutions every time they diagnose someone with a heart attack or a stroke. But implemented protocols in medicine DRAMATICALLY reduce negative outcomes, including DEATHS! In medical school, I had trouble remembering the acute treatment for an ST-Elevation Myocardial Infarction. Then someone taught me MONA-B: Morphine, Oxygen, Nitrates, Aspirin, Beta Blockers. Now, although I am an ophthalmologist, I STILL remember that protocol.

I beg you, make checklists a mantra for your business. Not only for the added benefit of consistency, accountability, scalability, and quality, but also because it is the single most significant component that you can IMMEDIATELY act upon and begin seeing dramatic results from.

- Dr. Timothy Johnson

5.3

THE THREE LEVELS OF ALL SUCCESSFUL
BUSINESS SYSTEMS

My friend, I have worked with thousands of successful companies and I want to clearly lay this out for you so that we do not have a bunch of pushback later.

Every successful and time freedom creating business that I have ever coached or observed has three levels of systems that support it.

- Layer 1 - The processes layer

- Layer 2 - The presentation layer

- Layer 3 - The "this is why we do it" layer

- Clay Clark

THE PROCESSES LAYER

The processes layer is basically all about the "check-this-box and do-that" to fulfill your practice's promises to patients. As an example, my super wife has some incredible recipes for creating some incredible organic and fruit-based smoothies that my kids love. The two times I followed her recipes and made the smoothies, the kids loved them. However, the other times I have produced smoothies on my own, my kids acted like a bee stung their tongues and they still talk about how terrible those smoothies were. There is a specific and right way to do things, and a wrong way to do things. To quote the R&B pop artist turned pastor, Montell Jordan, "This is how we do it." My friend, you have to document the super moves that you have developed that actually work.

- Dr. Timothy Johnson

THE PRESENTATION LAYER

The presentation layer is all about presenting your systems in a way that an honest human with a functional brain can follow. You will not believe how many times I have gone into a business to help them and have found that their checklists were so filled with jargon that no one had any idea what the crap was going on. In one specific situation, I went into a cosmetic surgeon's office and found jargon everywhere. "BVD, ACT, MVP, etc." I soon learned all of this jargon had been created by a man who no longer worked there. The business owner did not even understand the jargon! The staff just checked the boxes on the daily checklists to avoid getting in trouble. It was absolute jackassery (from the root word "jackass").

Think about Jiffy Lube or McDonald's. They have created repeatable systems so simple even my small brain could successfully execute them. When you go into Jiffy Lube they simply click from screen to screen and say, "Sir, your manufacturer recommends that you change your air filter every 'x' number of miles. Sir, your windshield wipers look as though they are worn. Sir, it looks as though your air coolant is low, however we can top that off for $4.00 today if you would like." I mean no disrespect when I say this, but those dudes get me for $176 every time I come in for the $19 oil change… and I love it! They have built a very effective presentation layer at Jiffy Lube. Go there and you will see what I am talking about.

- Clay Clark

NOTABLE QUOTABLE

"GOOD CHECKLISTS, ON THE OTHER HAND ARE PRECISE. THEY ARE EFFICIENT, TO THE POINT, AND EASY TO USE EVEN IN THE MOST DIFFICULT SITUATIONS. THEY DO NOT TRY TO SPELL OUT EVERYTHING--A CHECKLIST CANNOT FLY A PLANE. INSTEAD, THEY PROVIDE REMINDERS OF ONLY THE MOST CRITICAL AND IMPORTANT STEPS--THE ONES THAT EVEN THE HIGHLY SKILLED PROFESSIONAL USING THEM COULD MISS. GOOD CHECKLISTS ARE, ABOVE ALL, PRACTICAL."

Atul Gawande

(The bestselling author of *The Checklist Manifesto*, a surgeon and a professor of surgery at Harvard Medical School)

NOTABLE QUOTABLE

"GOOD MANAGEMENT CONSISTS IN SHOWING AVERAGE PEOPLE HOW TO DO THE WORK OF SUPERIOR PEOPLE."

John D. Rockefeller

(The self-made success story who went on to become the world's wealthiest man after having dropped out of high school to support his family)

As you are designing your presentation layer, keep your patients and your team members in mind. As you watch the systems in action, you must be 100% COMMITTED TO CREATING A REPEATABLE PROCESS THAT WORKS. Do not get emotional about your presentation. If your team cannot figure out your systems, keep redesigning them until anybody can figure them out. Actually watch your team try to implement your systems. If they cannot figure your system out, your system is too complex. Remember that the entire reason you are creating systems is to establish a scalable way to add value to your customers and make COPIOUS AMOUNTS OF MONEY to buy back your time.

 - Clay Clark

THE "THIS-IS-WHY-WE-DO-IT" LAYER

Writing about this layer irritates even me because I am a "shut-the-heck-up-and-put-your-head-down-to-get-the-job-done" kind of worker. Growing up with nothing, I have always viewed every job (since I became enlightened after reading Napoleon Hill's *Think and Grow Rich*) as a blessing and a gift, not as an obligation. I do speaking events all the time where the event planner asks me to do something that I do not want to do and I do it. Why? Because they are paying me $14,000. However, we are now at a point where the entitlement mentality of the average employee requires us to share the reason behind "why I am supposed to do this or that" now matters to many people. This layer really does matter to many employees and potential team members. This is why you and I must go out of our way to explain to team members why they are doing what they are doing.

Companies like Tom's Shoes, Warby Parker, and Whole Foods Market are winning in part because they connect with their team members on a deep and emotional level. Many of the employees really do buy into the vision of these companies and come to work motivated every day. Tony Hsieh of Zappos has assembled an army of people obsessed with offering the best customer service on the planet. You and I must inspire this same level of motivation from our teams. You must invest the time needed to explain to them why they need to follow your company's checklists and systems and once they connect with the sincerity of your purpose, most employees will want to come to work with you.   - Clay Clark

NOTABLE QUOTABLE

"BRANDING THROUGH CUSTOMER SERVICE OVER THE YEARS, THE NUMBER ONE DRIVER OF OUR GROWTH AT ZAPPOS HAS BEEN REPEAT CUSTOMERS AND WORD OF MOUTH. OUR PHILOSOPHY HAS BEEN TO TAKE MOST OF THE MONEY WE WOULD HAVE SPENT ON PAID ADVERTISING AND INVEST IT INTO CUSTOMER SERVICE AND THE CUSTOMER EXPERIENCE INSTEAD, LETTING OUR CUSTOMERS DO THE MARKETING FOR US THROUGH WORD OF MOUTH."

Tony Hsieh

(CEO of Zappos and the bestselling author of Delivering Happiness: A Path to Profits, Passion, and Purpose)

Quality people really want to thrive at work. Diligent people usually follow easy and practical systems and checklists. However, if your systems are too complex, your team members might improvise to meet your expectations without getting confused. They may "hack" their own version of your systems, which is not good.

- Dr. Timothy Johnson

5.4

BUILDING ONE CHECKLIST AT A TIME

As a man who has been self-employed for over 22 years and who has worked with thousands of clients, I have vast experience when it comes to seeing and personally doing what you shouldn't do. DO NOT TAKE A MONTH OFF FROM YOUR PRACTICE - SPEND THE VAST MAJORITY OF YOUR WORKING HOUR MAKING SYSTEMS, PROCESSES, AND CHECKLISTS.

The easiest way to make this change is to create systems as you see the need for them. Every time a team member does a repeatable process too slow or incorrectly, think about what you need to do to make the system more efficient. Every time an individual creates an excellent patient experience that surpass the quality of the average team member, document their methods. However always keep in mind, creating documents that no one uses is a waste of your time.

- Clay Clark

"DISCIPLINE IS THE BRIDGE BETWEEN GOALS AND ACCOMPLISHMENT."

Jim Rohn

(Bestselling author and renowned motivational speaker)

Building business systems is not an event but an ongoing process. Think of the process more like brushing your teeth than getting married. Unless you are a real sick freak, you are going to want to brush your teeth twice per day on an ongoing basis to maintain oral hygiene. On the flip side, unless you are a real sick freak, I do not recommend that you attempt to get married twice per day on an ongoing basis (I do not recommend you get married twice per day, ever). When you first start building your business systems, they are going to be very simple and incomplete. However, as you update these systems week-by-week, they will become the solid foundation upon which your company is built.

- Clay Clark

NOTABLE QUOTABLE

"SYSTEMS PERMIT ORDINARY PEOPLE TO ACHIEVE EXTRAORDINARY RESULTS PREDICTABLY."

Michael Gerber

(Bestselling author of the *E-Myth* book series)

5.5

INSTALLING THE GUARDRAILS

As your practice and your team ascends to Mount Awesome, you must work to ensure nobody on your team falls off the side of the mountain on the way to the top. To prevent your team members from falling off the mountain to their certain death, you must develop systems called GUARDRAILS. Guardrails are created to keep any one member of your team from ever being able to make a MASSIVELY COSTLY MISTAKE due to negligence, idiocy, carelessness, or just plain "JACKASSERY."

Years ago I worked with a doctor without guardrails. One employee's entire job was to "handle all of the finances for the business." When he deposited money in the bank, he redirected 5% of the practice revenue to his own account using a variety of quasi-clever and 100% illegal scams. Without exaggeration, this man deposited well over $500,000 of money within a year while embezzling around $25,000 for himself. He was ALSO allowed to use the company credit card without any oversight. Within a year, he had charged over $10,000 on personal purchases (most of which was spent at the local casino).

How was he eventually caught, you ask? When I was hired to improve the business systems for this doctor, I began setting up guardrails. When I insisted the same person should not deposit the money and reconcile the statements, this guy lost his mind. He pushed back, he attacked me, and asked repeatedly, "Why this guy not trust me?!" I calmly pointed out that we were simply setting up best-practice systems to avoid catastrophic errors in the future. These systems would reduce his stress and better secure his job and the practice. Within two weeks, the man submitted his resignation - just before we collected enough information to press charges.

- Clay Clark

Fun Fact:

75% of employees steal and most do so repeatedly."
(*Employee Theft: Are you blind to it* - CBS News:
https://www.cbsnews.com/news/employee-theft-are-you-blind-to-it/)

This is a true story and unfortunately, one that is repeated every day, all over the world, because companies lack proper guardrails. You must install reporting systems within your business to keep your team focused and on target. You may be wondering how you can possibly delegate more and more of the daily tasks of your business without completely losing control. Unless you just started your practice yesterday, you have probably witnessed the dangers associated with delegating key aspects of your business to a person on your team who screws up repeatedly. My friend, I want you to circle this and highlight this and do whatever you need to do to remember this statement: YOU WANT TO BUILD AND INSTALL SELF-REGULATING SYSTEMS INTO YOUR BUSINESS THAT ALLOW ETHICAL AND

DILIGENT PEOPLE TO GET THEIR JOB DONE RIGHT WITHOUT
EVERYTHING HAVING TO GO THROUGH YOU FIRST.

- Clay Clark

5.6

EXAMPLES OF EFFECTIVE
GUARDRAIL BUSINESS SYSTEMS

SYSTEMS provide transparency within your organization. Think of the UPS package tracking system. This system allows customers and UPS employees to locate a package. Think about the glass walls many high-end restaurants have installed so customers can see their food being prepared. Both of these systems hold employees accountable through transparency.

DASHBOARDS show the daily activity and results of each employee. Dashboards allow everyone within your organization to see the results delivered by each member of your team and hold everyone accountable.

CHECKLISTS create accountability by requiring the signatures of both the person completing the task and their manager.

FIXED EXPENSE AND VARIABLE EXPENSE BUDGETS are spreadsheets that allow you and your team to see where additional money is being spent outside the pre-agreed financial boundaries.

SCORECARDS AND SCOREBOARDS are charts that show everyone the performance, statistics, conversion rates; and quality control scores eliminate finger pointing and highlight the top performers.

STANDARDIZED AND COMPLIANT CONTRACTS allow you to engage in the same type of transaction over and over again. It makes sense to implement a standardized contract. Over the years I have worked in commercial real estate, photography, entertainment, speaking, consulting, membership-based medical care, and countless other fields, and cannot stress enough the importance of having standardized and compliant contracts. See ThrivetimeShow.com/testimonials for thousands of video testimonials from the great business people like you whom I've helped. In 2019, my average client grew by 104%. Don't believe me? Check out ThrivetimeShow.com/does-it-work.

OFFICIAL POLICIES AND PROCEDURES provide a company Process for handling complaints, refunds, mistakes, and customer service issues will save management a ton of time putting out small fires by empowering your team to make good decisions to satisfy your customers.

"THERE IS ONLY ONE BOSS. THE CUSTOMER. AND HE CAN FIRE EVERYBODY IN THE COMPANY FROM THE CHAIRMAN ON DOWN SIMPLY BY SPENDING HIS MONEY SOMEWHERE ELSE."

Sam Walton

(Co-founder of Wal-Mart/Sam's Club)

Years ago, I worked with a retail business in which thousands of transactions took place per week. Less than 2% of the customers were ever upset, but you could almost guarantee that the owner was going to be called and asked how to handle nearly 40 customer service issues per week (2,000 transactions x 2% = 40 customer service issues). He could not get ahead because he was dealing with a customer service issue nearly every hour of the day as his business was open over 50 hours per week.

We empowered his staff to give up to a 100% refund to any dissatisfied customer. When they installed the L.A.S.T. (Listen Answer Satisfy Trust) system for dealing with customer complaints, guess what? The staff resolved 38 out of 40 issues per week directly and customers got an immediate solution to their problems. Because the members of his team were instructed to bring L.A.S.T. forms to the weekly management meeting, the owner was aware of customer service issues.

This small change allowed the man to become a proactive business owner once again. BOOM! - Clay Clark

....

Definition Magician:
"BOOM!" is an Acronym that stands for:
Big **O**verwhelming **O**ptimistic **M**omentum

....

AUTOMATED BACKUPS automatically back up every digital file daily. You would not believe how many businesses owners have lost every digital file because one personal computer failed. I highly recommend Dropbox.com. Dropbox.com allows you to access any file from anywhere at any time. I have developed a file nomenclature for both internal and external use. I highly recommend you implement it now so that you no longer have to waste time hunting for mission critical files and passwords. To learn more about our naming system, simply email us today at info@thrivetimeshow.com.

If you build these GUARDRAILS properly, you will safeguard your business systems and dramatically decrease the number of decisions you need to make each day. This will unleash your company's growth and dramatically improve your mental health. I am not kidding when I say mental health. Drake Baer wrote for Business Insider "The scientific reason why Barack Obama and Mark Zuckerberg wear the same outfit every day."

He writes that many top leaders including Steve Jobs, President Obama, and Mark Zuckerberg wear the same or similar outfits every day to reduce 'decision fatigue.'"

"HE (STEVE JOBS) DID NOT WANT TO MAKE A DECISION ABOUT WHAT TO WEAR SO HE WORE THE SAME THING. THAT IS ABOUT FOCUS. IT IS ABOUT DECIDING WHAT THINGS YOU ARE GOING TO FOCUS ON AND HE KNEW THAT WAS ONE ITEM THAT HE COULD PEEL AWAY FROM HIMSELF TO TAKE AWAY THE CLUTTER. WELL THAT SAME THING...I SAW HIM DO ALL DAY EVERY DAY."

Tim Cook

(Current CEO of Apple)

NOTABLE QUOTABLE

"'YOU WILL SEE I WEAR ONLY GRAY OR BLUE SUITS,' [OBAMA] SAID. 'I AM TRYING TO PARE DOWN DECISIONS. I DO NOT WANT TO MAKE DECISIONS ABOUT WHAT I AM EATING OR WEARING. BECAUSE I HAVE TOO MANY OTHER DECISIONS TO MAKE.' HE MENTIONED RESEARCH THAT SHOWS THE SIMPLE ACT OF MAKING DECISIONS DEGRADES ONE'S ABILITY TO MAKE FURTHER DECISIONS."

Michael Lewis

("*Obama's Way*," Vanity Fair, October 2012)

Read more about decision fatigue at:

http://www.businessinsider.com/barack-obama-mark-zuckerberg-wear-the-same-outfit-2015-4

http://www.cnn.com/2015/10/09/world/gallery/decision-fatigue-same-clothes/index.html

http://www.nytimes.com/2011/08/21/magazine/do-you-suffer-from-decision-fatigue.html?_r=0

5.7

UNLOCKING YOUR PRACTICE'S FAST AND SUSTAINABLE GROWTH POTENTIAL BY LISTENING TO YOUR CUSTOMERS

Years ago I spoke at a business conference in Florida on the importance of listening to your current customers to create additional opportunities. These opportunities meet your customers needs through solving additional problems that they have by upselling. I asked the audience to rate on a scale of 1 to 10 the effectiveness of their current systemic and checklist-driven upselling processes. A dentist approached me after my talk to say he could dramatically increase his sales if he just knew how to create upselling systems.

We started by asking every one of his current and former patients which other dental related services they had purchased in the past year. We discovered that nearly 30% of his 500 former and current patients over the past five years had paid for teeth whitening, Invisalign teeth straightening, or cosmetic veneers. We discovered that many of his patients did not know that his practice offered these cosmetic services. We also discovered that practically none of his patients knew that he provided long-term financing through the third-party medical financing company CareCredit.

When we reviewed these findings, the dentist's mind almost exploded at the thought of the easy business (low-hanging fruit) he let slip through the cracks. His current patients were going to other dental offices for services and financing options that he currently offered! After the dentist emotionally recovered, he implemented a checklist at check-out to educate every patient about the services and financing options his practice provided. This one move increased his sales by nearly 35%. Like this dentist, most companies do not systematically cross-sell and up-sell in such a way that every single customer knows about every single product and service that you offer every single time. This must happen or you are leaving tons of money on the table.

- Clay Clark

5.8

IDENTIFY YOUR IDEAL AND LIKELY BUYERS, FIND THEIR NEEDS, AND SELL THEM SOLUTIONS

For massive success, you must sit down and identify your ideal and likely buyers. No, not every human with a pulse who lives within a certain distance of your business is an ideal and likely customer. And no, you cannot say, "If we just get 1% of every person in China to buy our product...." Once you have clearly identified your ideal and likely buyers, focus on which of these buyers will pay you the quickest. Medical professionals can quickly put together a profile of ideal and likely patients by identifying the following:

- The gender of your ideal and likely buyers _____

- The age of your ideal and likely buyers _____

- The publications that your ideal and likely buyers consume (trade journals, magazines, blogs, podcasts, etc)_____

- The hobbies enjoyed by your ideal and likely buyers _____

- The stores and online retailers routinely visited by your ideal and likely buyers _____

- The net worth of your ideal and likely buyers_____

- The value of the home of your ideal and likely buyers _____

- The geographic locations of your ideal and likely buyers _____

- The job title of your ideal and likely buyers _____

- The connections, networks and key industry influencers who interact with your ideal and likely buyers _____

- The social circle of your ideal and likely buyers _____

- The schools the children of your ideal and likely buyers attend ___

_____

- Clay Clark

5.9

DR. TIM'S PRESCRIPTION FOR SUCCESS:
ENGAGE YOUR IDEAL AND LIKELY BUYERS

As you begin to grow your practice, you must develop an intimate understanding of your ideal and likely patients. This does not just mean studying trends, measuring numbers, and creating graphs. GO TALK TO THEM. You must install listening posts and touch points into your patient experience until you dial in your scalable model. Think about the length of the experience your customer has with your practice. While your touch points may only exist for 5-10 minutes on the phone or in-person, the customer experience may last hours, days, weeks, months, or years with your practice. It is important that you make the experience as high-touch as needed to learn at an expedited rate, while starting a business and dialing in who your ideal and likely patients are. Go meet your ideal and likely patients. Call them frequently to check on their experience. Send them unsolicited thank you notes. Build a relationship with them. This is one of the best returns on investment for a fledgling business. At the core of every medical business is people. If you are struggling to figure out how to solve a problem for the entire business, think about what you would imagine to be an over-delivery moment in your work-flow and attempt to WOW in that situation. Come back later and figure out how to make the excellent patient care and customer service that provide repeatable and scalable solutions.

- Dr. Timothy Johnson

NOTABLE QUOTABLE

"IT IS EASIER TO LOVE A BRAND WHEN THE BRAND LOVES YOU BACK."

Seth Godin

(The marketing expert and best-selling author
of the book *The Purple Cow* and the man who sold his company
Yoyodyne to Yahoo! for a rported $30 million)

5.10

IDENTIFY YOUR MAIN COMPETITORS AND THEN TAKE THE FOOD OUT OF THEIR MOUTHS

NOTABLE QUOTABLE

"IT IS NOT SUFFICIENT THAT I SUCCEED; EVERYONE ELSE MUST FAIL."

Larry Ellison

(The billionaire CEO of Oracle with whom you may not agree, but with whom you may be competing)

You need to know your competition more intimately than they know themselves, or they are going to beat the crap out of you in the marketplace.

To make sure you do not get discouraged by your competitors, I encourage you to write down your biggest Strengths, Weaknesses, Opportunities, and Threats, known as the SWOT analysis. I also recommend that you ask:

• Which top four competitors already sell to your ideal and likely buyers? _____

- Which indirect competitors do your ideal and likely buyers turn to for products and services they need outside of your direct competitors?

  _____

- How did your top four competitors acquire your ideal and likely buyers? _____

- What are the strengths of your top four competitors? _____

  _____

- What are the weaknesses of your top four competitors? _____

  _____

- What opportunities exist to beat the crap out of your top four competitors? _____

- What threats do your top four competitors face? _____

  _____

- Why do you dislike your top four competitors (if you do not have any, that is OK; but I doubt that is the case)? _____

  _____

- Why are you motivated to beat the crap out of your top four competitors? _____

  _____

- How are your top four competitors' websites better than yours? ___

  _____

- What about your top four competitors' marketing materials is better than yours? _____

  _____

- What niches in the market are not currently being dominated by your competition (best price, best cheerleader, really friendly, best customer service, easiest to use, easiest to order, best tasting, most interactive, most customized, best experience)? _____

  _____

- Who is going to mystery shop (code for spying) your top four competitors? _____

  _____

- What is your marketing plan to beat your top four competitors? (in two sentences or less)? _____

  _____

- What is your plan to offer a better product and service experience for your ideal and likely buyers than is currently being offered by your top four competitors? _____

  _____

- Clay Clark

"BUY OR BURY THE COMPETITION."

Jack Welch

(Former CEO of GE whom many consider to be the
best CEO of his time)

I once coached a Dallas-area-based attorney who reached out to me after reading an article I published on Entrepreneur.com. He was absolutely being killed by another attorney in the marketplace. I led him through the questions listed in this section. We hired some people (you could call them spies) to enlist the services of his competition and quickly realized how his competition was getting his business and out-performing him in nearly every way. Within 60 days, we developed a strategic plan to beat the living daylights out of his competition. Within 12 months, we did just that. You may think that I am a little dramatic when I say, "killing the competition" and "spying on your enemies," but I promise you that if you are not spying on your competition, they will eat your lunch, your customers, and half of your potential income.

My friend, Netflix and Amazon absolutely destroyed Blockbuster by redefining the way people rent movies. iTunes came into the industry and devastated the CD manufacturing business. Uber is taking massive quantities of business away from taxi drivers. Airbnb is decimating the hotel industry in many cities. I took my wife away from a dude she was dating at the time (true story and I still feel very proud of this achievement). My friend, you have to ask yourself this question: Who is the Darth Vader capable of absolutely destroying your industry?

Most businesses have had no clue about the evil Darth Vaders and outside trends that are coming to destroy their business models and their means of supporting their families and fulfilling their dreams. Unless you want to get hit by an industry-destroying bus, you need to identify major disruptions so you can pivot your business model, if needed. - Clay Clark

---

NOTABLE QUOTABLE

"FACE REALITY AS IT IS, NOT AS IT WAS OR AS YOU WISH IT TO BE."

Jack Welch

(Arguably the most successful CEO of his era as the CEO of GE who grew the company 4,000% during his tenure)

To prevent yourself from being run over by an industry-destroying bus, take the time to answer the following questions:

- What are the four biggest industry-destroying buses that are headed your way? _____

  _____

- What will you have to do if these industry-destroying buses collide with you and your business? _____

  _____

Now that you have a good understanding of how you stack up versus the competition, it is very important to formalize your observations into a visual tool that you can use to help you beat the living daylights out of your competition. Today is the day that you must buy that HUGE WHITE BOARD you have always dreamed of. Literally, you need to buy a massive white board today. But do not buy one from an office supply place. Go to Home Depot or Lowes and buy shower board for 1% the cost of a white board. Boom! This book just saved you hundreds of dollars on white board. Watch - "How to Make a 4x8 Dry Erase Board for $20." https://www.youtube.com/watch?v=8r6Lm1y_diY

- Clay Clark

5.11

DR. TIM'S PRESCRIPTION FOR SUCCESS:
ONLY THE PARANOID SURVIVE

Andy Grove was the chairman of Intel during its great transition from memory to microprocessors. He detailed this transition in his fantastic book, *Only the Paranoid Survive*. You NEED to be paranoid. I am an ophthalmologist. I am always looking for the next disruption. In-office cataract surgery? Robot surgery? Drops to dissolve cataracts? I have contingency plans for each of them. I do not care what your specialty is. Someone, somewhere is trying to make you obsolete. Do not let them.   - Dr. Timothy Johnson

5.12

FIND THE MARKET'S NEED AND FILL IT IN A
MEMORABLE AND DIFFERENTIATED WAY

My friend, revenue comes from filling a market need in a memorable and differentiated way. Imagine you own a sporting goods store next door to Walmart. How would you beat Walmart? You cannot beat them on pricing. Walmart buys in such volume that you would not stand a chance. To beat Walmart, your sporting goods store would have to provide a super-wide variety of specialty sporting goods items and a Disney-level customer experience. Then you could actually compete with Walmart and beat them in the sporting goods niche. To win in business, you must find your niche.

If you are stuck searching for your niche, look at the intersection of these four areas:

- Your company's biggest strengths

- Your competition's biggest weakness

- Your target market's needs

- Your core competency (the product or service your company can scalably provide)

Once you find the need in the market that you can fill better than anyone else in the world, you will become known for this. Think about the following brands. - Clay Clark

Really take a moment and mentally marinate on the following brands:

Zappos - This company, founded by Nick Swinmurn, focused on building the world's first major online shoe retailer with a focus on offering free returns, a huge selection of shoes, and incredibly high levels of customer service. In 1999, Nick reached out to Tony Hsieh to help him scale his concept. Tony joined Zappos as their new CEO in 2000 when the company did approximately $1.6 million in sales. By 2009, Zappos revenues had reached $1 billion in annual sales.

Airbnb - This company was started in October of 2007 in San Francisco by Brian Chesky and Joe Gebbia. They focused on offering short-term living quarters for people who would rather experience staying at a local person's residence as opposed to staying in a corporate hotel chain. By 2010, there were 15 people working from Chesky and Gebbia's loft apartment (their home office). The company continued gaining traction. Then, in November 2010, they raised $7.2 million from Greylock Partners and Sequoia Capital, having booked 80% of their total 700,000 bookings in just the past six months.

Starbucks - Howard Schultz joined the existing company called Starbucks with a vision to create a "third place" for people who appreciate coffee and want to gather with others to connect and enjoy coffee at a place that had an ambiance and warmth that would make people want to linger in conversation. He focused on making sure that Starbucks customers came there as much for the experience as they did for the coffee itself. To create this experience, he insisted on incorporating intentionally beautiful decor, intentional smells, intentional music, and intentional nomenclature. He made sure that the people who made the coffee were named very differently from the competitors. Starbucks does not offer small, medium, and large coffees like everyone else. They offer tall, grande, and venti sizes.

To win in the game of business, you must "be the first or second best in something." You must find a niche that you can absolutely dominate and then you can start finding more ways to solve the problems of the ideal and likely patients in that niche. If you are stumped and you do not know what niche you can fill, I recommend finding 15 ideal and likely patients and asking them all the same question:

"As it relates to your medical niche, what company first comes to mind when you think of _____ (your unique niche)?"

If everyone you talk to keeps immediately mentioning Zappos or Starbucks, you may need to rethink your unique niche and value proposition. You must find a way to generate a product by offering products and services that your ideal and likely patients want in a way that is currently not being served by your competition.

- Clay Clark

NOTABLE QUOTABLE

"MAKE SURE THAT EVERYBODY IN YOUR [COMPANY] COMES TO WORK EVERY DAY TRYING TO FIND A BETTER WAY. YOU HAVE TO ABSOLUTELY LOOK OUTSIDE, INSIDE, [AND] KNOW THAT SOMEBODY IS DOING IT BETTER THAN YOU AND YOU HAVE GOT TO DRIVE THAT INTO EVERY PERSON IN YOUR ORGANIZATION. 'THERE IS A BETTER WAY OF DOING THIS, DAMN IT, FIND IT!' YOU MAY BE NUMBER ONE, BUT YOU ARE ONLY NUMBER ONE FOR AS LONG AS THE SNAPSHOT [IN TIME] AND SOMEBODY IS ALWAYS SHOOTING AT YOU. SO THIS IS A DRIVE THAT PEOPLE HAVE TO COME WITH."

Jack Welch

(The legendary former CEO of General Electric)

5.13

BRANDING 101

The billionaire businessman and entrepreneur behind PayPal, Tesla, SpaceX, Solar City, etc, Elon Musk described branding best: "Brand is just a perception, and perception will match reality over time. Sometimes it will be ahead, other times it will be behind. But brand is simply a collective impression some have about a product."

Your brand is simply what people think about your company. The only way to brand (sear) an idea into the brains of your ideal and likely buyers is to focus on the results you provide your customers and the emotional connection you want your ideal and likely buyers to have with your products. Once you know what your brand is and who your ideal and likely buyers are, it is very important that you brand your company properly by consistently doing the following three things right:

Always have your ideal and likely patients in mind when you do any marketing. Ask yourself what message will resonate most with your ideal and likely patients.

- Never do any branding or marketing that will cause your ideal and likely patients to lose trust in you and your brand.

- Mentally marinate on the following examples of great branding at work. When most people think of the following brands, what do they think about?

Apple

1. It works.

2. It is designed with function and style in mind.

3. It is innovative and different.

Southwest Airlines

1. They are fun.

2. They have consistently low fares.

3. They will not hit you with any hidden fees.

Disney

1. It is a magical and happy place for families.

2. It offers good clean fun.

3. It is epic and everything about it is always done on a grand scale.

Alright, now we need to take a moment to think about your practice. How do people think about your brand? The Walt Disney Company focuses on providing a good clean enjoyable family environment. Undoubtedly at some point, someone associated with the company probably found a niche they could dominate if they moved slightly away from that focus. In fact, Disney attempted this, but did so under the separate brand Miramax so as not to taint their Disney brand. Southwest Airlines is focused on providing low fares but without a doubt, at some point somebody within the company probably suggested they could make a quick profit with a few extra fees. Apple was the love of Steve Jobs' life, but he was actually fired from the company in part for defending the brand. Once he was fired, the company shifted to offer a ton of products that did not work well because they were bogged down with features customers did not want. They had to bring Jobs back to fix the brand before it went under.

- Clay Clark

"THE PRODUCTS SUCK! THERE'S NO SEX IN THEM ANYMORE!"

Steve Jobs

(Co-founder of Apple commenting on Apple's products before his return to Apple in 1997)

Now roll up your sleeves and get to work defining the promises you will make to your customers. Consider the emotions you want them to feel. Consider your customer's experience as it relates to your business. Turn your ideas into a visual using that new white board of yours to keep your company focused. Take a moment to define the overall experience, the sights, the sounds, the smells, the interactions, and the emotions you want your customers to have when engaging with your brand. Take a moment to obsess about the profound C.R.A.P. (Creates Revenue, Repeatable, Actionable, Profitable) found on the following pages.

In order to turn your Branding Experience Worksheet into reality, you are going to need to create detailed checklists for each aspect of your branding experience with a quality control / accountability loop to ensure that the "brand promise" you make to your customers is never compromised.   - Clay Clark

5.14

THE CUSTOMER WILL ONLY PAY FOR AN
EXPERIENCE THEY WANT

Now before you start getting "too mystic" about those elements of the branding experience you want the customer to enjoy, please understand that the patient is the boss. You must allow the patient and their emotional and practical needs to dictate how you brand your business. Imagine you open up a quick oil change and car maintenance business and your daughter is obsessed with princesses. You decide to brand your quick oil change and car maintenance business based upon her love of princesses. You may be in for a rude awakening and a bad reception from your customers. Perhaps your customers will appreciate the fact that your team of technicians is wearing pink and the "Nutcracker Suite" is playing overhead at all times.

However, if they do not understand how the theme works in conjunction with the products and services you are offering, you cannot be offended or completely unwilling to accept feedback from the customer. You must provide a product, service and brand that your ideal and likely buyers love.

- Dr. Timothy Johnson

NOTABLE QUOTABLE

"THERE IS ONLY ONE BOSS. THE CUSTOMER. AND HE CAN FIRE EVERYBODY IN THE COMPANY FROM THE CHAIRMAN ON DOWN, SIMPLY BY SPENDING HIS MONEY SOMEWHERE ELSE."

Sam Walton

(American businessman and entrepreneur best known for founding the retailers Walmart and Sam's Club)

6.1

IDENTIFY AND DESTROY YOUR BUSINESS'
BIGGEST LIMITING MEMBRANE

In every business, yes EVEN IN MEDICINE, limiting membranes cause your practice to become stagnant. As the owner of the business, you must always ask yourself what single largest factor is capping the growth of your business? What one thing, if you just could get your hands on it, fix it, or move it out of the way, would be a game-changer for your business? Which critical hire would take your business to the next level almost immediately? My friend, you must DEEP DIVE into asking yourself these questions with great intensity.

Once you have identified your biggest limiting factor, you must now list out a minimum of 10 possible solutions to eliminate this problem. After you have done this, you want to ask yourself which of these ideas is a game-changer and which of these potential solutions is effective and quickly doable.

Once you have identified the effective and quickly doable items, you must assign who is going to take action, when they need to have it done, and what resources they need to get the job done. Accountability is key and usually encounters massive pushback from the people being held accountable. Many people immediately think change will lead to the elimination of their job. As the CEO, reassure them and teach them why improvement is important.

Now as for those game changers, we are not going to forget about them. Game changers have the ability to do just that; they can change the game and take your company, your income, and your life to the next level. However, game changers typically take a ton of time to implement and they also have the potential to blow up and never come to fruition due to complexity of implementing them. Thus, you are going to want to assign weekly action items focused on executing the game changer, but not at the expense of missing out on the immediate wins and quick successes that could easily be produced by knocking out a few of the quickly doable items. - Clay Clark

---

NOTABLE QUOTABLE

"OFTEN ANY DECISION, EVEN THE WRONG DECISION, IS BETTER THAN NO DECISION."

Ben Horowitz

(Self-made billionaire and co-founder of both
Opsware which he sold to Hewlett-Packard for $1.6 billion in cash)

6.2

OPPORTUNITY COST 101

If you will pardon me, I am going to go a little deeper into the world of entrepreneurship than most doctors are comfortable with. Here's the scoop. On Planet Earth, we all only have 24 hours per day at our disposal. Entrepreneurs tend to be very aware of this fact, while the majority of people in the world seem unaware of this concept. Effective entrepreneurs grasp the reality that they have a finite amount of time, but an unlimited number of choices and ideas. To become an effective entrepreneur, YOU MUST BECOME OBSESSED WITH BEING THE MOST EFFECTIVE MANAGER OF TIME ON THE PLANET. You must become very good at gathering all the facts and repeatedly saying no to good, average, or terrible things so that you can focus on the most fruitful action items for both you and your organization.

- Clay Clark

"PEOPLE THINK FOCUS MEANS SAYING YES TO THE THING YOU HAVE GOT TO FOCUS ON. BUT THAT IS NOT WHAT IT MEANS AT ALL. IT MEANS SAYING NO TO THE HUNDRED OTHER GOOD IDEAS THAT THERE ARE. YOU HAVE TO PICK CAREFULLY. I AM ACTUALLY AS PROUD OF THE THINGS WE HAVEN'T DONE AS THE THINGS I HAVE DONE. INNOVATION IS SAYING NO TO 1,000 THINGS."

Steve Jobs

(Co-founder of Apple and the former CEO of Pixar)

Repeat after me: time is your most valuable resource… time is your most valuable resource… time is your most valuable resource…. Constantly evaluate your commitment to things that make the highest and best use of your limited time. Occasionally you may want to schedule a leadership retreat with your team or step away from the daily battle yourself to really analyze where your company is headed. Ensure you are truly directing your company to offer the most value to your customers and ensure the most profits for you.

- Clay Clark

NOTABLE QUOTABLE

> "THE ART OF LEADING COMES DOWN TO ONE THING:
> FACING REALITY, AND THEN ACTING DECISIVELY AND
> QUICKLY ON THAT REALITY."

Jack Welch

(The former CEO of GE who grew the company
by over 4,000% during his tenure)

. . . .

Fun Fact:

"(Steve) Case (AOL Founder) says that he does
not remember the total amount spent on the discs
specifically, but says that in the early 1990s, AOL's
goal was to spend 10 percent of lifetime revenue to
get a new subscriber. He says that since the average
subscriber life was around 25 months, revenue was
about $350 off of each of these users. So he guesses
they probably spent about $35 per user on things such
as these discs."

"*How Much Did It Cost AOL To Send Us Those CDs
In The 90s? 'A Lot!,' Says Steve Case.*" - MG Siegler in
Tech Crunch

. . . .

"EVERY TIME YOU MAKE THE HARD, CORRECT DECISION YOU BECOME A BIT MORE COURAGEOUS, AND EVERY TIME YOU MAKE THE EASY, WRONG DECISION YOU BECOME A BIT MORE COWARDLY. IF YOU ARE CEO, THESE CHOICES WILL LEAD TO A COURAGEOUS OR COWARDLY COMPANY."

Ben Horowitz

(Self-made billionaire and co-founder of Anderson-Horowitz venture capital)

6.3

DR. TIM'S PRESCRIPTION FOR SUCCESS: STRATEGICALLY THINK ABOUT YOUR CAPABILITIES

You MUST evaluate the capabilities of your team on an ongoing basis. Commit, right now, to learning and making on-going improvement part of your practice's culture. Each week obsess about improving your practice by 2%. Your company's ability to learn will determine whether or not you are able to adjust to the ever-changing landscape of the market over time. Likewise, your company's capability as a whole is dictated by the skills that your employees possess.

Which "black hole" of skills exists within your company (meaning which skills are in short supply or missing entirely)? Begin planning to shore up those areas. This may be an excellent opportunity for you to evaluate the growth of individual employees who have proven themselves and may be ready for more responsibility.

6.4

GETTING STUFF DONE WITH QUARTERLY EXECUTION PLANS

Alright, I know we have discussed a lot up to this point. I hope that your brain has not yet exploded as we have defined who our ideal and likely buyers are, what niche we are focused on, the importance of systems, and the importance of working on your business and not just in your business. Now we need to actually start executing your big vision to turn your plans into reality.

NOTABLE QUOTABLE

"SIMPLE CAN BE HARDER THAN COMPLEX. YOU HAVE TO WORK HARD TO GET YOUR THINKING CLEAN TO MAKE IT SIMPLE."

Steve Jobs

(The guy who co-founded Apple and the former CEO of Pixar who helped launch the first completely computer animated box office hit, *Toy Story*)

6.5

LET'S GET SIMPLE

My friend, your ability to turn your dreams and ideas into reality is going to come down to your ability to direct your daily calendar and your team's calendar towards the achievement of your quarterly goals, while continuing to deal with the daily challenges involved in running a business. Having a quarterly focus is ideal, as it breaks down your big-vision action items and stretch goals into manageable pieces. Break down your quarterly goals into weekly action items that must be completed, and hold your team accountable for knocking out their action items by the assigned deadlines. A quarterly outlook provides a long enough period of time for you to get large quantities of work done, bringing you closer to the achievement of your big, hairy, audacious goals.

───────────────┤ NOTABLE QUOTABLE ├───────────────

"RARELY DO WE FIND MEN WHO WILLINGLY ENGAGE IN HARD, SOLID THINKING. THERE IS AN ALMOST UNIVERSAL QUEST FOR EASY ANSWERS AND HALF-BAKED SOLUTIONS. NOTHING PAINS SOME PEOPLE MORE THAN HAVING TO THINK."

Martin Luther King, Jr.

(An American Baptist Minister best known for his role in leading the civil rights movement in the United States based on his non-violent Christian beliefs)

6.6

BREAK DOWN YOUR BIG GOALS INTO ROLLING DAILY ACTIONABLE ITEMS (TO-DO LISTS) FOR YOUR TEAM

This step is where the magic really begins to happen. If nothing gets scheduled, nothing gets done. If massive goals are not broken up into specific step-by-step action items, then nothing will get done, either. You and your leadership team must become proficient at breaking down big goals into small daily action steps. So that I do not leave you with only a vague understanding of this HUGELY IMPORTANT CONCEPT, I am going to let you peek behind-the-scenes when my team and I opened up Elephant in the Room Store #2 at 91st and Yale in Tulsa, Oklahoma. - Clay Clark

Story Time:

The big goal was to get Store #2 into the profit zone within 90 days of opening, and we did it. This is a partial look at the marketing to-do list that made it happen.

Elephant in the Room – Michael design Valpak mailer (see Clay for verbiage) – Due Monday – 7/29

Elephant in the Room – Michael design targeted online ads (see Clay for verbiage) – Due Monday – 7/29

Elephant in the Room – Michael design landing page (see Clay for verbiage) – Due Monday – 7/29

Elephant in the Room – Tonya reach out to Valpak to determine the cost of mailing 30,000 men who live within three miles of the 91st and Yale Location 2. Only mail to homes worth more than $300,000 – Due Monday – 7/29

Elephant in the Room – Jonathan – Write press release announcing dollar give-back to the Tulsa Boys Home for every haircut we provide – Due Monday – 7/29

Elephant in the Room – Jonathan set up Twilio account to mass text entire database of clients about new location (see Clay for verbiage) – Due Monday – 7/29

Elephant in the Room – Jonathan create mass email to be sent out via Constant Contact to every client in our database (see Clay for verbiage) – Due Monday – 7/29

Elephant in the Room – Jonathan design online targeting ad demographic – Due Monday – 7/29

Elephant in the Room – Devin populate the Twilio database with customer information – Due Monday – 7/29

Elephant in the Room – Devin populate the Constant Contact database with customer information – Due Monday – 7/29

Elephant in the Room – Clay proof Valpak mailer – Due Monday – 8/1

Elephant in the Room – Clay proof targeted online ads – Due Monday – 8/1

Elephant in the Room – Clay proof landing page – Due Monday – 8/1

Elephant in the Room – Clay proof Valpak costs for mailing 30,000 men who live within three miles of the 91st and Yale Location 2. Only mail to homes worth more than $300,000– Due Monday – 8/1

Elephant in the Room – Clay proof press release announcing dollar give back to the Tulsa Boys Home for every haircut we provide – Due Monday – 8/1

Elephant in the Room – Clay proof Twilio account to mass text entire database of clients about new location – Due Monday – 8/1

Elephant in the Room – Clay proof mass email to be sent out via Constant Contact to every client in our database – Due Monday – 8/1

Elephant in the Room – Clay proof online targeting ad demographic– Due Monday – 8/1

Elephant in the Room – Clay proof the Twilio database with customer information – Due Monday – 8/1

Elephant in the Room – Clay proof the Constant Contact database with customer information – Due Monday – 8/1

NOTABLE QUOTABLE

"MAKE EVERY DETAIL PERFECT, AND LIMIT THE NUMBER OF DETAILS TO PERFECT."

Jack Dorsey

(Co-founder of Twitter and Founder of Square)

As you can intuitively sense, most people do not like this part. Everyone likes to make money, few enjoy creating a linear and detailed plan filled with small achievable actionable items. Disorganized entrepreneurs tend to have a rude awakening when they discover that the most successful entrepreneurs are the ones who are the most organized and well planned. At this point, wantrepreneurs usually say to me, "But I thought if I just believed it and was motivated enough, that money would just jump into my wallet from the "Law of Attraction."

- Clay Clark

NOTABLE QUOTABLE

"IN THE ABSENCE OF PROCESSES THAT CAN GUIDE PEOPLE, EXPERIENCED PEOPLE NEED TO LEAD. BUT IN ESTABLISHED COMPANIES WHERE MUCH OF THE GUIDANCE TO EMPLOYEES IS PROVIDED BY PROCESSES, AND IS LESS DEPENDENT UPON MANAGERS WITH DETAILED, HANDS-ON EXPERIENCE, THEN IT MAKES SENSE TO HIRE OR PROMOTE SOMEONE WHO NEEDS TO LEARN FROM EXPERIENCE."

Clayton M. Christensen

(Author of *How Will You Measure Your Life?* American scholar, educator, author, business consultant, and religious leader who currently served as the Kim B. Clark Professor of Business Administration at the Harvard Business School)

6.7

TIME MANAGEMENT MASTERY SUPER MOVES

Now that you are equipped with a fire hose of knowledge, action items, and steps to build a more scalable business, you may be wondering, "How in the world am I going to implement all this?" IT IS GOING TO TAKE TIME. Most business owners are so busy working IN their businesses that they rarely have time to work ON their businesses. On those rare occasions when they finish their work at a respectable hour when the sun is still out, they are usually too exhausted to deep dive into creating documents, systems, and processes, which all require close attention to detail. By scheduling time to work ON your business, you will slowly begin to transition your business to one that can operate without your direct involvement. However, just like any other appointment, if you do not put it on your calendar, it will not get addressed.

Business owners who are already working 70, 80, or 90 hours per week in their business cannot stomach the thought of tacking on an additional three hours per day to work ON their business. Well, take heart! I have provided you with Super Moves that will free up the needed time to work ON your business.   - Clay Clark

Time Management Mastery Super Move #1 - Blow up items on your to-do list. You must become very comfortable saying "no" to things other people try to put on your to-do list. When someone says, "Call me and remind me to do this or that," you need to respond in a nice tone of voice, "I believe in your ability to remind yourself and if you cannot, I am not going to be responsible for reminding you to do things." - Clay Clark

NOTABLE QUOTABLE

"THIS IS NOT ABOUT MANAGING YOUR TIME. IT IS ABOUT KEEPING YOUR LIFE UNDER CONTROL. PLAN THE LIFE YOU WANT OR LIVE THE LIFE YOU DO NOT WANT."

Lee Cockerell

(Former Executive Vice President of Walt Disney World Resorts who once managed 40,000 employees and 1,000,000 guests week)

Delete that funk. Many times activities get e-mailed to you or put on your calendar and you just need to delete that stuff. Every day, I get an e-mail from a person telling me that I need to call them back about A,B, and C because of X,Y, and Z. If the person is not my wife, one of my business partners, or a customer, I simply delete that funk.

Do not do anything. Sometimes people want to give me updates about updates and everything that is being communicated has zero impact on my life or the status of our business. This basically describes the agenda of a typical networking event. Some dude makes some announcement about some esoteric legislative bill that does not directly impact you, and then some other dude in a suit talks in generalities about the state of the economy, and then some sincere lady talks about her vision for a cleaner community. As for me and my wallet, we are not going to sit through those gatherings just so I can pass out my business card to the 76 multi-level marketing professionals, three realtors, and two insurance agents in attendance.

Delegate it. There are many things that you should delegate. In my office, I am always asked to get involved in stupid stuff that does not matter. The decision of whether to order our paper towels online or directly from Office Depot is one such instance. True, if we order them online, they will take longer to arrive, but if we buy them direct from Office Depot, our paper towel budget will be about $4.00 per week more. Seriously? This is something I should delegate to somebody who is empowered to make the decision while protected by the "guardrails" we wrote about in Sections 4 and 5. This person knows what paper towels should cost and knows that it is not acceptable to ever run out. If the person in charge of the paper towels shows that they do not have the mental capacity to make this decision, then I need to find a new paper towel ordering person. Do not embroil yourself in stuff that does not make highest and best use of your time.

Create a system enhancement that makes the repetitive questions disappear forever. If every customer asks you where the restroom is, it is probably because the sign identifying your customer restroom is not visible enough. Lee Cockerell, former executive vice president of Disney World Resort, once told me about how much time Disney had invested to ensure that the signage at their properties is clear and obvious. The people at Disney World see over one million guests per week, so they knew they had to create systems designed to make repetitive questions disappear forever or everyone would spend their entire vacation asking where the bathrooms and the gifts shops were.

- ClayClark

NOTABLE QUOTABLE

"BE WHO YOU ARE AND SAY WHAT YOU FEEL, BECAUSE THOSE WHO MIND DO NOT MATTER AND THOSE WHO MATTER DO NOT MIND."

Dr. Seuss

(Bestselling children's author and illustrator who sold over 600 million copies of his books before his death)

• **Time Management Mastery Super Move #2 - Stop listening to the feedback of people who are not your ideal and likely buyers and**

who are not truly experts - Most people do not like their lives and do not have successful businesses, thus you should not listen to most people regarding your practice. Simply ignore people who are negative or become an excellent selective listener. - Clay Clark

Fun Facts:

"85% of job applicants lie on their resume"
- *Inc. Magazine* | *https://www.inc.com/jt-odonnell/staggering-85-of-job-applicants-lying-on-resumes-.html*

"75% of US employees steal from the workplace"
- US Chamber of Commerce

• **Time Management Mastery Super Move #3 - Ordain your destiny daily** - Each day when you first wake up, look at your to-do list (not your text messages, your social media updates, or your e-mail) and write down the items that you definitely will accomplish that day. Then schedule time to accomplish those tasks. When you begin your day by ordaining your destiny, you will find yourself becoming DRAMATICALLY MORE EFFICIENT, FOCUSED, AND EFFECTIVE.

• **Time Management Mastery Super Move #4 - You must block out time every week for your highest and best use activities only.**

If you cannot keep from being distracted in your office, you need to work from your truck, a hotel, the middle of a forest, or anywhere other than my Man Cave (which is where I will be). Do whatever it takes to block out the time for your highest and best use activities.

Turn your phone off, turn your e-mail off, and get it done. When I first met David Robinson (the NBA Hall of Famer), I was shocked to discover that he had multiple cell phones, until he told me that one is for his wife and kids and the other one is for everybody else (myself included). This was smart because as a two-time Olympic gold medal winner, NBA Champion, and former MVP who has since gone on to become a big-time investor in a $300 million investment fund (The Admiral Fund), his phone never stops ringing. He had to find a way to create clear boundaries for himself and by having two cell phones, he was able to do that. - Clay Clark

---

NOTABLE QUOTABLE

"A PERSON'S SUCCESS IN LIFE CAN USUALLY BE MEASURED BY THE NUMBER OF UNCOMFORTABLE CONVERSATIONS HE OR SHE IS WILLING TO HAVE."

Tim Ferriss

(Bestselling author of *The 4-Hour Work Week*, venture capitalist and podcaster)

• **Time Management Mastery Super Move #5** - Create an "I am going to stop doing this" list. I run into so many people who keep doing things because they have always done them. You must start delegating or deleting things from your list if you ever hope to move on to doing bigger and better things.

Just because you have always done something does not mean that you have to keep doing it. If you are having routine computer issues, accounting issues, human resource issues, or other issues, you must be committed to making changes, regardless of whether they are uncomfortable or not.   - Clay Clark

6.8

UNLOCKING THE POWER OF DISCIPLINED TIME MANAGEMENT

Whenever I speak to our 500,000 listeners on our daily ThrivetimeShow.com podcast about the importance of disciplined time management, people look at me with the same face as if you were about to disclose all of the sins they have ever committed. Do not freak out about disciplined time management. In fact, I encourage you to greatly simplify this idea in your mind because it is not as overwhelming as advertised. At the end of the day, disciplined time management comes down to a few variables:

1. Right Time of Day - Make sure that you are working at the right time of day. For me, I simply cannot get things done while my teammates, their emotional baggage, their questions, their joy, their pain, and their issues of the day swirl all around me. I must plan my day from 3:00 AM to 9:00 AM. This is what I call my "meta time." It is the time each day when I can truly think above and beyond my current circumstances and can get massive quantities of work done. I mean this. For me personally, I am writing this book LITERALLY at 4 AM while listening to the soundtrack to The Last Samurai with zero interruptions.   - Clay Clark

Definition Magician:

The word "Meta" comes from the Greek word meaning "after" "beyond" or "higher."

NOTABLE QUOTABLE

"LACK OF DIRECTION, NOT LACK OF TIME, IS THE PROBLEM. WE ALL HAVE TWENTY FOUR-HOUR DAYS."

Zig Ziglar

(Bestselling author and renowned motivational speaker)

2. Right Environment - Make sure that you are working in the right environment. I am writing this book from within the beautiful confines of my speakeasy-themed Man Cave. This room is almost sacred to me, a place where I can shut off the outside world, crank up the bagpipe music that I often listen to, and just get it done. Back in the day before I could afford to build a speakeasy-themed Man Cave, I worked in my apartment with my phone off and with headphones on to escape interruptions. - Clay Clark

---

NOTABLE QUOTABLE

"CONCENTRATE ALL YOUR THOUGHTS UPON THE WORK AT HAND. THE SUN'S RAYS DO NOT BURN UNTIL BROUGHT TO A FOCUS."

Alexander Graham Bell

(Inventor of the world's first modern telephone)

3. No Distractions - Make sure that you turn off all distractions. As I write, I am celebrating my 38th consecutive hour of having my phone turned off. I do not check e-mails, I do not answer the door, I just crank up my bagpipe music, epic movie scores, and I get stuff done. I am not interested in social media updates or who may be calling, I am just 100% focused on writing the best business book for medical professionals so that you can change your life and so that I can fulfill my mission to mentor millions.

4. Accountability - Make sure that you insert accountability into your life. It is important that you have a business coach or business partner who holds you accountable. If you can achieve success without a business coach or partner in your life, then you are a better businessperson than Steve Jobs (the co-founder of Apple), Eric Schmidt (the CEO of Google), and Jeff Bezos (the founder of Amazon), all students of the legendary business coach Bill Campbell who kept them focused, accountable, and moving forward.

Everybody needs someone to keep them on track and hold them accountable for hitting deadlines, getting stuff done, and not letting emotions get in the way of the perpetual motion needed to achieve big time business success. Our one-on-one business coaching program has limited availability (160 clients), but to learn more about it, visit ThriveTimeShow.com. - Clay Clark

Fun fact:
"96% of business fail within 10 years."
- *Inc Magazine* - https://www.inc.com/bill-carmody/why-96-of-businesses-fail-within-10-years.html

In 2019 our average client grew their business by 104%. See their stories by visiting ThrivetimeShow.com/does-it-work

NOTABLE QUOTABLE

"EVERYONE NEEDS A COACH."

Bill Gates

(Co-founder of Microsoft giving a TED speech in April of 2013)

---

5. Boundaries - Set boundaries with your time. Thousands of people reach out to me each month. I work with great customers who write super positive things about our brands and me on social media. Then there are other people who hate me for standing up for my core beliefs, firing someone they are married to, firing their son, driving a Hummer, etc. It would be easy to get overwhelmed if I stayed updated about the mindless and meaningless media swirling around me. It is up to me to set up boundaries in my life for when I will check social media, check e-mail, answer my phone, etc. It is up to me to decide when I will be involved in a business meeting and when I will not be. I have to set my own boundaries. - Clay Clark

"WE NEED TO RE-CREATE BOUNDARIES. WHEN YOU CARRY A DIGITAL GADGET THAT CREATES A VIRTUAL LINK TO THE OFFICE, YOU NEED TO CREATE A VIRTUAL BOUNDARY THAT DID NOT EXIST BEFORE."

Daniel Goleman

(Psychologist and bestselling author of *Emotional Intelligence*, who has been a guest on the *ThriveTime Show* podcast)

Set boundaries with the people with whom you choose to engage. People do not deserve your time simply because they request it, or because they are related to you, or because they live near you. In fact, if you did have to say yes to every person who ever asked for a minute of your time, you would not ever become successful. Once you start to achieve any level of success at all, more and more people will begin reaching out to you and requesting moments of your time. I have had to become increasingly good at saying no to time-sucking, negative, reactive, and pessimistic people, or people I just do not like.

- Clay Clark

6.9

DR. TIM'S PRESCRIPTION FOR SUCCESS:
CONTROL ACCESS TO YOU

I really do not like pharmaceutical reps who show up at my office, unannounced, and expect me to stop seeing paying patients to allow them to sell me on their product. Who approved this system? I made a rule in my office that unless reps schedule a patient appointment, they are not allowed to see me. My time, as well as my patients' time, is too valuable. — Dr. Timothy Jonson

6.10

LEARNING TO MANAGE YOUR DISTRACTIONS
(SOCIAL MEDIA, E-MAILS, TEXT MESSAGES,
MISSED CALLS, ETC)

Having been self-employed for so long, I no longer struggle with saying no to things; however, I used to. Therefore, I am going to attempt to empathize while being very pragmatic as I lay out the rules you need to implement in your life to better manage your e-mail, your social media, your text messages, and the constant distractions that people with less intentional life plans are using to try to slow you down.

— Clay Clark

NOTABLE QUOTABLE

"YOUR E-MAIL, TEXT MESSAGE, AND SOCIAL MEDIA IS YOUR TO-DO LIST THAT YOU ARE ALLOWING TO BE MADE BY OTHER PEOPLE. DO NOT LET IT CONTROL YOUR LIFE. SET BOUNDARIES OR SPEND YOUR DAY RESPONDING TO RANDOM-ASS UPDATES OF YOUR COUSIN WHO WAS OFFENDED THAT YOU DID NOT RESPOND TO THE PICTURE THEY TAGGED YOU IN ON FACEBOOK OR INSTAGRAM."

Clay Clark

(The former U.S. Small Business Administration Entrepreneur of the Year, host of the 6x iTunes chart-topping podcast, the founder pf DjConnection.com, EITRLounge.com, EpicPhotos.com, MakeYourLifeEpic.com, etc)

NOTABLE QUOTABLE

"SOCIAL MEDIA WASN'T INVENTED TO MAKE YOU BETTER – IT WAS INVENTED TO MAKE THE COMPANIES MONEY. YOU ARE AN EMPLOYEE OF THE COMPANY AND YOU ARE THE PRODUCT THAT THEY SELL. THEY HAVE PUT YOU IN A LITTLE HAMSTER WHEEL AND THEY THROW LITTLE TREATS IN NOW AND THEN – BUT YOU HAVE GOT TO DECIDE, WHAT IS THE IMPACT YOU ARE TRYING TO MAKE?"

Seth Godin

(The bestselling author, entrepreneur, marketing expert, and *ThrivetimeShow.com* podcast guest)

Inform your sales team that you expect customer service and sales emails to be handled in real time and inboxes to be at zero at the end of the day. Educate and inform your clients and your staff that henceforth, you (as the leader) are only going to be checking your email once each morning. Quit responding to social media unless it pays you to do so. My wife and I live on land behind a wall with a forest right behind our house, but I do not feel a psychological urge to run into the woods and pick up a branch every time one falls from the hundreds of trees. However, I used to feel the need to respond to every social media update involving me. What a fruitless waste of time.

If you insist on responding to all social media, also make sure to invest the time needed to respond to all physical mailers and cold-calls too.

- Clay Clark

Fun Fact:

"You do not really need science to know this, but technology makes it much easier to get distracted, whether that is stepping away from an important project to check your smartphone, or flipping between multiple browser tabs without really focusing on any one. It has been proven that toggling between multiple tasks at once does not actually work — in fact, you just wind up performing all your duties even worse... No, 'Internet addiction' is not just some BS term parents throw around to terrify youngsters who spend too much time playing Candy Crush. Spending too much time on the Internet can actually cause changes in the brain that mimic those caused by drug and alcohol dependence, according to a 2012 study."

"*8 Ways Technology Makes You Stupid*" *The Huffington Post*
https://www.huffpost.com/entry/technology-intelligence_n_5617181

"BE PRESENT. BE MEDITATIVE. FORM REAL FRIENDSHIPS."

Naval Ravikant

(Founder of AngelList.com and successful venture capitalist)

Disconnect your social media from your smart phone updates. Every time someone writes about you, tags you, messages you or reaches out to you, you do not need to know. Constantly interrupting your train of thought with the random updates from potentially hundreds of thousands of people out there who have the ability to reach you at any time can cause you real psychological damage. Seriously. Harvard, Yale, and other leading schools have done research on what happens when a person has to make too many decisions during a workday and their findings are not positive. - Clay Clark

Fun Fact:

American adults spend over 11 hours per day listening to, watching, reading, or generally interacting with the media."
- Nielsen (7/31/2018)

Start the subject line of an email with the name of company or the main person involved in the email. Do not send blank or vague subject lines.

To reduce the number of e-mails that you receive every day, you must reduce the number of e-mails that you send every day.

As a leader, do not respond to your email in real-time. Respond to all of your email once per day and then get the heck out of there. If you are in a position of leadership, you will lose your mind trying to stay on top of it in real-time.

Do not engage in nuanced conversations via email. Reserve those types of conversations for in-person or over-the-phone.

Do not send long emails.

Do not criticize people in emails, especially group emails.

When possible, respond to long emails filled with many questions with the answer, "I will call you about these items ASAP." Then make sure to cover all of the items in the email during your phone conversation.

Write your emails using numbered bullet points when discussing multiple issues. Do not weave many questions and subjects into the body of an email paragraph. If you believe that the topic of your email may be very sensitive to the reader or that it may actually offend or upset the reader, do not send it.

Do not ever write something in an email that you would not be willing to say directly to the person. Get your inbox reduced to zero each day. Do not leave hundreds of half-responded to or not responded to emails in your inbox. Commonly use the carbon copy (CC) feature on your email, but never use the blind copy (BC) feature on your email, if possible. - Clay Clark

---

NOTABLE QUOTABLE

"WHEN PEOPLE THINK OF MENTAL ACTIVITY, THEY TEND TO THINK OF IT AS AN ETHEREAL/ZAPPING OF ELECTRICITY THAT HAS NO COST TO THE BODY. THAT IS NOT TRUE, THE BRAIN IS A MASSIVE BLOOD AND OXYGEN SINK. YOU NEED STIMULUS AND RECOVERY IN MENTAL WORK IN THE SAME WAY THAT YOU NEED STIMULUS AND RECOVERY FOR SPORTS."

Tim Ferriss

(Venture capitalist, podcaster, speaker, entrepreneur and bestselling author of *The 4-Hour Workweek* book series)

6.11

You have the time you need to create repeatable business systems that will create both time and financial freedom for you. I have had countless business people come up to me and say, "I would love to grow my business, but I just cannot find the time." And they are 100% wrong, 100% of the time. I would guess that you are already putting in the hours needed to take your business to the next level. However, you can incrementally increase the value of each hour of your working day by upgrading the way you use your time through creation of the systems and processes you need to grow. If you need accountability, one-on-one coaching and a team to support you. Schedule your 13-point assessment with me by visiting ThrivetimeShow.com.

Growing your business in a duplicable way is not an event. It will not happen with the touch of a button or with the brief placing of a call. We can help you completely change your life if you will allow us to guide you through the process of executing the best-practice systems that you have learned throughout this book.   - Clay Clark

6.12

WHAT ARE THE FIRST THINGS
YOU SHOULD BE DOING?

To help you get some big and quick wins and to establish a renewed sense of momentum within your company, I have put together a list of the FIVE BIGGEST action items you need to implement within the next week. Each one of these action items will take less than 25 minutes to implement, but you must commit to doing them for them to work.

- Clay Clark

"Nothing works unless you do."

Maya Angelou

(Award-winning actress, poet, and civil rights leader)

6.13

ACTION ITEM #1: DEFINE AND CLARIFY YOUR PERSONAL F6 GOALS (FAITH, FAMILY, FINANCES, FRIENDSHIPS, FITNESS, AND FUN)

It is almost impossible to drift your way to success. You will not push back against outside pressures, your peers, and the culture around you if you do not know where you want to go. Invest the time to type in and print out your F6 Goals today.

When you print out those goals, place them somewhere so that you can see them in the morning when you wake up, during the day when you are working, and at night when you go bed. You can get to where you want to go if you will only invest the time to define where it is that you want to go. - Clay Clark

---

NOTABLE QUOTABLE

"DRIFTING, WITHOUT AIM OR PURPOSE, IS THE FIRST CAUSE OF FAILURE."

Napoleon Hill

(Bestselling self-help author and the former apprentice of the
world's wealthiest man, Andrew Carnegie)

6.14

ACTION ITEM #2

DEFINE YOUR IDEAL AND LIKELY BUYERS

You must invest the time needed to create a document that clearly identifies who your ideal and likely buyers are and who they are not. This will save you thousands of dollars down the road in fruitless marketing efforts and it will impact nearly every business decision that you make. - Clay Clark

6.15

ACTION ITEM #3:

DETERMINE THE COSTS ASSOCIATED WITH ACHIEVING YOUR IDEAL LIFESTYLE

It is great to have massive goals, but you must really get out the calculator, a pen, and paper to figure out how much your goals are really going to cost you monetarily during each year. If you want to get in shape, gyms are not free. If you want to get engaged but have yet to convince your fiancé that your engagement shouldn't involve the purchase of diamond ring simply because De Beers executed a brilliant marketing strategy that has now convinced the world's market that a man who is proposing to a woman must invest his hard-earned money into buying her a diamond ring if he truly cares about her and the relationship, getting engaged is not free. Food is not free. Most things in life are not free. So you must create a business that exists to serve you and provide you with the time and financial freedom needed to afford your ideal lifestyle.

....

Fun Fact:

Today, the De Beers Group of Companies seems to be the most magical company in the diamond industry. They play a leading role in the diamond exploration, diamond mining, diamond trading, diamond retail sales and the industrial diamond market. However, 1938 is when the magic really began. De Beers hired the N.W. Ayer advertising agency to help make diamonds appeal to a broader audience. Ayer felt that the company needed to link the purchase of a diamond to something emotional to keep the sale of diamonds from going up and down during predictable economic cycles. He recommended that the company begin advertising diamonds as something that men should buy and give to women when proposing and getting married. According to the *New York Times*, Ayer told everyone on his team that he wanted to "create a situation where almost every person pledging marriage feels compelled to acquire a diamond engagement ring." Before World War II, less than 10% of engagement rings contained diamonds. However, once Ayer began marketing the phrase "A Diamond Is Forever" on all of De Beers' advertisements beginning in 1948, it became almost a given that men will buy their brides to be a diamond ring. And who came up with the idea that a man should save up two months of salary to buy a diamond ring before proposing? You guessed it; it was Ayer.

6.16

ACTION ITEM #4:

DETERMINE YOUR HIGHEST AND BEST USE

TO SCALE YOUR COMPANY

My friend, you and I are where we are because of how we spend our time. If you want to upgrade your life, you will need to upgrade how you manage your time. We encourage you to explore the Time Management System created by Lee Cockerell (former Executive Vice President of Walt Disney World Resort) and the trainings related to it, available at Thrive15.com so that you can start leveraging your time more efficiently. Lee was able to successfully manage over 40,000 cast members while working at Disney, not because he was a genius, but because he had learned how to become a maniacally focused efficient manager of time. We all only have 24 hours in a day and it is time for you to really focus on optimizing how you invest that time.

- Clay Clark

┌─────────────────────────┐
│   NOTABLE QUOTABLE   │
└─────────────────────────┘

"YOU EITHER PAY NOW OR PAY LATER WITH JUST ABOUT EVERY DECISION YOU MAKE ABOUT WHERE AND HOW YOU SPEND YOUR TIME."

Lee Cockerell

(The former Executive Vice President of Operations of Walt Disney World Resort)

6.17

ACTION ITEM #5

Subscribe to the *Thrivetime Show* podcast on Spotify, iTunes, or iHeart Radio and commit to investing 15 minutes a day to listen and learn how to grow a successful business and how to build a successful life.

In his exhaustive study of the habits of the rich, Tom Corley (Bestselling author of *Rich Habits – The Daily Success Habits of Wealthy, Thrivetime Show* guest, CPA, and the founder of www. RichHabitsInstitute.com) discovered some incredible habits that the rich seem to almost universally have, many of which involve the ongoing pursuit of self-improvement and business mastery.

- ✔ 88% of wealthy read 30 minutes or more each day for education or career reasons vs. 2% of poor.

- ✔ 67% of wealthy watch one hour or less of TV every day vs. 23% of poor.

- ✔ 44% of wealthy wake up three hours before work starts vs. 3% of poor.

- ✔ 84% of wealthy believe good habits create opportunity luck vs. 4% of poor.

- ✔ 86% of wealthy believe in lifelong educational self-improvement vs. 5% of poor.

Stanford Professor Carol S. Dweck wrote a bestselling book focused on what makes people successful called, *Mindset: The New Psychology of Success* (Ballantine Books, 2007). In her book, she says, "Mindset change is not about picking up a few pointers here and there. It is about seeing things in a new way. When people...change to a growth mindset, they change from a judge-and-be-judged framework to a learn-and-help-learn framework. Their commitment is to growth, and growth takes plenty of time, effort, and mutual support."

My friend, I do not want to say that you will be a pathetic loser if you do not commit to blocking out 15 minutes per day for ongoing education and business training on a consistent basis, but it is a fact. You will lose if you do not invest the time needed to study proven systems, strategies, and processes. - Clay Clark

Phase #4

"YOU HAVE GOT TO FIND WHAT YOU LOVE. AND THAT IS AS TRUE FOR YOUR WORK AS IT IS FOR YOUR LOVERS. YOUR WORK IS GOING TO FILL A LARGE PART OF YOUR LIFE, AND THE ONLY WAY TO BE TRULY SATISFIED IS TO DO WHAT YOU BELIEVE IS GREAT WORK. AND THE ONLY WAY TO DO GREAT WORK IS TO LOVE WHAT YOU DO. IF YOU HAVEN'T FOUND IT YET, KEEP LOOKING. DO NOT SETTLE. AS WITH ALL MATTERS OF THE HEART, YOU WILL KNOW WHEN YOU FIND IT. AND, LIKE ANY GREAT RELATIONSHIP, IT JUST GETS BETTER AND BETTER AS THE YEARS ROLL ON. SO KEEP LOOKING UNTIL YOU FIND IT. DO NOT SETTLE.

Steve Jobs

(Co-founder of Apple and the founder of NEXT, and the former CEO of Pixar)

7.1

OPTIMIZE YOUR PERSONAL HAPPINESS AND PERSONAL LIFE SATISFACTION

It is vitally important that you love your daily schedule, even if you do not love providing the medical care you have been trained to provide. We have seen many business owners who do not follow the principles that have been outlined throughout this book, and eventually they become a hostage of their own organization. Do business the way YOU want to do business, not the way that your customers or employees want to do it. You are going to spend an extraordinary amount of time with your business, so take care to develop a good relationship with it. Without developing goals for your 6 F's (Faith, Family, Finances, Friendships, Fitness, and Fun), the rigors and challenges of operating and growing the business will be your only daily focus.

You are given one life to do great things, and that is not isolated to doing only great things in business. You are empowered to great things in each of your Six F's. Develop an incredible faith. Be the most healthy person possible so you can live long enough to reap the rewards of your labor. Spend time with family. Build relationships with genuine people. Create wealth in abundance. Growth in these areas not only moves you forward toward your goals, but it also enhances your balance and satisfaction. We have seen many business owners neglect one or more of these areas for too long and become unbalanced, discouraged, and dissatisfied with their business. There are certainly seasons where the focus will shift between each of the Six F's, but the important thing is to not lose sight of any of them entirely. The easiest way to do this is to remind yourself every day of each of your goals. Through achievement and progress, you will find balance and satisfaction.

- Clay Clark

"LIFE IS LIKE RIDING A BICYCLE. TO KEEP YOUR BALANCE, YOU MUST KEEP MOVING."

Albert Einstein

(The brilliant mind responsible for saving our country by alerting President Franklin Delano Roosevelt to the certain doom that would face America if the Nazis were allowed to create the first nuclear bomb)

7.2

SUCCESS IS WORTH IT

Growing up, I never thought I would become the U.S. Small Business Administration Entrepreneur of the Year for the great state of Oklahoma, or that I would become the successful founder of several multi-million dollar businesses. I still remember the first time I was asked to entertain for a high-class venue (remember, I was a DJ in my early career). I still remember the first time I deposited $2,000 of profits into the bank after a fun weekend of entertaining. I can still remember what it felt like the first time I was able turn back on the air-conditioning unit at our one-bedroom apartment because we had the money to afford the electric bill. I can still remember how it felt the first time www.DJConnection.com hit $1,000,000 in annual sales. I still remember how it felt when Elephant in the Room hit $1,000,000 in annual sales. I still remember what it felt like the first time I got asked to speak to a group of people. My friend, whatever your goals are, achieving success is worth it.

But I do not want to put my goals on you. Maybe being debt-free and living in a van down by the river is your vision of success and that is OK. My mission to mentor millions is centered around helping those millions live the life of their dreams during this brief period of time we all get to experience on Planet Earth.

This book is intended as a primer for business education for medical professionals. Hopefully it has stirred inside you a desire to master your medical practice and the ability to achieve your life goals If you do the following: - Clay Clark

ACTION ITEMS

1. Pass on what you've learned by writing a Google Review. search for "ThriveTime Show Jenks" on Google Maps and write a review today!

2. Don't miss a radio show or podcast. Subscribe on iTunes at ThriveTimeShow.com.

3. Get all of the interactive downloadables by signing up today at ThriveTimeShow.com.

WANT MORE?
Check out the Ultimate Textbook for Starting, Running & Growing Your Own Business!

Start Here

NEVER before has entrepreneurship been delivered in an UNFILTERED, real and raw way... until now. This book is NOT for people that want a politically correct and silver-lined happy-go-lucky view of entrepreneurship. That's crap. Supported by case studies and testimonials from entrepreneurs that have grown their businesses all over the planet using these best practice systems, former U.S. Small Business Administration Entrepreneur of the Year, Clay Clark, shares the specific action steps for successful business systems, hilarious stories from situations that every entrepreneur faces, and entrepreneurship factoids that are guaranteed to blow your mind.

Invite a Friend to Join You at the World's Best 2-Day Intensive Business Workshop

Get specific and practical training on how to grow your business

www.ThriveTimeShow.com/Conference

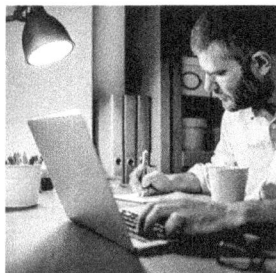

WANT ONE-ON-ONE MENTORSHIP AND BUSINESS COACHING?
VISIT WWW.THRIVETIMESHOW.COM/COACHING
Let our team help you execute your action items and guide you down the proven path (see ThriveTimeShow.com)

DID YOU KNOW THAT MY CHART-TOPPING THRIVETIME SHOW PODCAST HAS FEATURED SUCH GUEST AS:

THOMAS GOLISANO
The billionaire founder of Paychex

JOHN MAXWELL
8x New York Times Best-Selling Author and Leadership Expert

WOLFGANG PUCK
Celebrity Chef, Entrepreneur, and New York Times Best-Selling Author

GUY KAWASAKI
Legendary Former Key Apple Employee Turned Venture Capitalist, Best Selling Author

SHARON LECHTER
New York Times Best-Selling Co-Author of Rich Dad Poor Dad

CRAIG GROESCHEL
Senior pastor of the largest church in America with over 100,000 weekly attendees (Lifechurch.tv)

DAVID BACH
One of America's most trusted financial experts and has written nine consecutive New York Times bestsellers with 7 million+ books in print

DAVID ROBINSON
NBA Hall of Famer (2-time NBA Champion, 2-time Gold Medal Winner)

ZACK O'MALLEY GREENBURG
Senior Editor for Forbes and 3x Best-Selling Author

JOHN LEE DUMAS
Most Downloaded Business Podcaster of All-Time (EOFire.com)

SETH GODIN
New York Times Best-Selling Author of Purple Cow, and former Yahoo! Vice President of Marketing

ADAM BERKE
Co-Founder of the 700+ Employee Advertising Company (AdRoll)

MARY ANN ZOELLNER
Emmy Award-winning Producer of the Today Show and New York Times Best-Selling Author of Sh*tty Moms

JONAH BERGER
New York Times Best-Selling Author
of Contagious: Why Things Catch On and
Wharton Business Professor

DAN HEATH
New York Times Best-Selling Author
of Made to Stick and Duke University
Professor

TOM PETERS
International Best-Selling Author of In
Search of Excellence

MUGGSY BOGUES
NBA Player and Coach (Shortest player to
ever play in the league)

RASHAD JENNINGS
NFL Running Back (and Winner of Dancing
with the Stars

LEE COCKERELL
The former Executive Vice President of Walt
Disney World who once managed 40,000
employees)

MICHAEL LEVINE
PR consultant of choice for Michael
Jackson, Prince, Nike, Charlton Heston,
Nancy Kerrigan, etc.

COLTON DIXON
Billboard Contemporary Christian Top 40
Recording Artist

BEN SHAPIRO
Conservative Talk Pundit, Frequent Fox News
Contributor, Political Commentator and Best-
Selling Author

According to *Business Insider*, 90.8% of people use Google to search for the products, services, and medical care they need thus I thought I should include a game-changing bonus for you.

So without any further ado, I've included both chapters 1 & 2 of our amazon bestselling book. Search Engine Domination:

The Proven Plan, Best Practices, Processest super moves to make millions with Online marketing.

STEP #1
Create a website with the proper Google compliant website architecture.

STEP #4
Gather objective Google reviews from your customers.

STEP #3
Set up and optimize your Google My Business Map / listing.

STEP #2
Create a website that is Google mobile compliant.

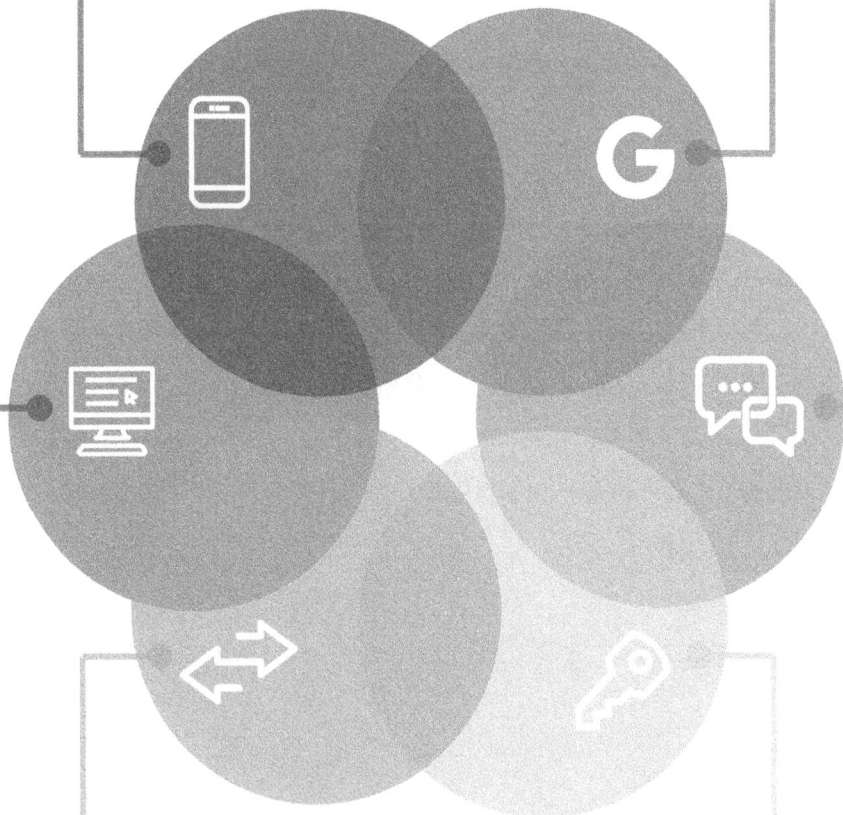

STEP #6
Generate the most high-quality backlinks possible.

STEP #5
Create the most relevant and keyword-rich original content possible.

```
<header class="chapter-title">
    <p>CHAPTER 1</p>

    <h1>
```

SEARCH ENGINE DOMINATION

```
    </h1>
</header>
```

```
<style>
    #page-background{
        background-color: #F4B400;
    }
        .chapter-title p{
            text-transform: uppercase;
            color: white;
            font-family: 'Proxima Nova';
            font-weight: 600;
        }

        .chapter-title h1{
            text-transform: uppercase;
            color: white;
            font-family: 'Proxima Nova';
            font-weight: 900;
        }
</style>
```

Everyone Uses the Internet, Yet Few Know How to Market Effectively Using It.

According to research published by Pew Research in March of 2018, 77% of people now go online on a daily basis to find the answers, solutions, products, services and connections they are looking for. However, from both our personal experience and having worked with thousands of people to help them to increase their companies' value by hundreds of millions of dollars, I have personally discovered that less than 1% of the clients that we have worked with knew how search engine optimization truly worked before we taught it to them.

During the pages of this practical, action-orientated, and game-changing book, we will teach you the specific steps that you need to take in order to begin generating leads and making money as a result of learning how to dominate search engine results.

> "Almost 90% of consumers said they read online reviews."
>
> **- FORBES**
>
> ("Online Reviews And Their Impact On The Bottom Line")

Search engines are used by the vast majority of people to find the products and services that they buy, yet very few people truly understand how search engines actually work.

Search engines use electronic devices commonly referred to as "spiders," "robots" (or "bots") to crawl and scan the vast internet in search of the most relevant content that they can display to search engine users.

The Most Relevant Original HTML Content + The Most Objective Reviews + The Most Mobile Compliance + The Most Google Compliance = Million$

In order to do this, search engines "index", "catalogue," and "sort" the information that is publicly available on the internet so that when a user conducts a search using a search engine they are able to find the information that is most relevant to their search terms.

In fact, here is an explanation of how Google works from Google itself, "The software behind our search technology conducts a series of simultaneous calculations requiring only a fraction of a second. Traditional search engines rely heavily on how often a word appears on a web page. We use more than 200 signals, including our patented PageRank algorithm, to examine the entire link structure of the web and determine which pages are most important. We then conduct hypertext-matching analysis to determine which pages are relevant to the specific search being conducted.

By combining overall importance and query-specific relevance, we're able to put the most relevant and reliable results first. (Corporate Information, Google).

NOTABLE QUOTABLE

"Success is a choice."

- NAPOLEON HILL

(Best-selling self-help author of all time)

Organic Search 101: 🌿

Most of the people on the planet who choose to use search engines to find the products, services, and solutions that they are looking for, are not inclined to sift through pages and pages of search engine results to find the result that they believe to be the best. In fact, most users refuse to ever even consider the search results found on page 2 of most Google search engine results. In years past, on other search engines, you could just pay to have your website ranked higher on search engine results, but Google decided to change everything and created the absolute best search engine results possible for users when they decided to not allow businesses to "pay to play" as it relates to dominating organic search engine results (although you can buy advertisements using Adwords).

Google's founders Larry Page and Sergey Brin leveled the playing field for people like us that did not grow up with silver spoons in our mouths when they decided to fill the majority of their search engine results with non-paid search engine results and content that was created by diligent people who were actually willing to invest the time needed to create Google compliant websites and content.

Design 101:

You must obsess over the concept that your website only exists to provide solutions for your ideal and likely buyers and to help you make a profit as a result of providing those solutions to your ideal and likely buyers. Many business owners spend every dime that they have on creating a visually incredible website that

> "If you can't explain it simply, you don't understand it well enough."

· ALBERT EINSTEIN

(Albert Einstein was the German-born theoretical physicist that saved America. The Nazis were very close to developing nuclear bombs that they were committed to dropping on United States soil when Albert Einstein alerted our American President Franklin Delano Roosevelt of the diabolical technological advances. Only after much pleading did President FDR agree to allow America to begin investing the resources and the time needed to create our game-changing nuclear weapon at the last hour. In 1921, Einstein won the Nobel Prize in Physics.)

no one can ever find because it does not follow Google's search engine compliance rules.

Clay has personally employed and fired well over a dozen web-developers who refused to grasp this concept because of their fascination and preoccupation with building websites that were visually incredible and virtually undiscoverable by search engines.

The Google Domination Equation

Proper Google Website Architecture (must follow Google's canonical rules) + Proper Google Mobile Compliance + Reviews + Most Relevant Original Content + Most High Quality Backlinks = Top of Google Search Engine Results.

The bottom line is that the sites that have the most overall Google canonical compliant architecture, the most Google mobile compliant architecture, the most original relevant content and the most relevant, high quality backlinks, will win. Once you wrap your mind around this idea, you can win. However, before you can win, you must first know what search terms (also referred to as "keyword phrases") are actually winnable.

How to Determine Winnable Keywords

As an example, let's say you want your website to come up in the top of the Google search results for the search term, "San Diego Dog Training." To help you to determine if this search term is actually winnable, we will now walk you through the process.

STEP 1: Type "San Diego Dog Training" into the Google search bar and hit enter. After you skip past the Adwords, and the 2 Yelp listings, Johnknowsdogs.com currently comes came up top in the search results.

No Jonathan Kelly does not own JohnKowsDogs.com.

STEP 2: Go to SEMRush.com. SEMRush.com allows you to run a website audit on your competitor's website so you can see how they are doing (JohnKnowsDogs.com got a score of 78% and SEMRush will tell you why). It will also tell you the top keywords that JohnKnowsDogs.com is ranking for, what sites are linking to JohnKnowsDogs.com, and any ads that JohnKnowsDogs.com is running.

STEP 3: Go to https://www.google.com/webmasters/tools/mobile-friendly/ and run a report on their overall Google mobile compliance score. Unfortunately, while the page is mobile friendly, there are some issues.

STEP 4: Go to freetools.webmasterworld.com/ and click on "Indexed Pages" to determine how many pages of content the johnknowsdogs.com people have. Currently

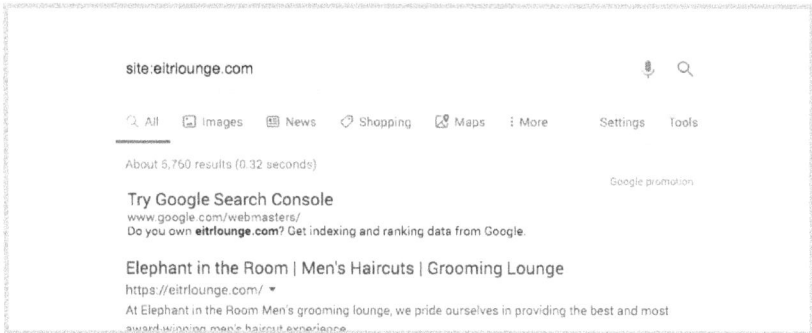

they have 67 pages of content on their website that are indexed in Google (Google requires each page to have 350 + words or more). Internally we require our team to write 1,000 words on each page of the websites we write search engine optimization content for. Another way to check is to take their URL and simply add "Site:" in front of the website address. **Example: Site:Eitrlounge.com**

STEP 5: Go to developers.google.com/speed/pagespeed/ insights/ to check your website speed. On mobile, JohnKnowsDogs.com has a page speed score of 88%.

Equipped with this information, you now know that if you wanted to beat JohnKnowsDogs.com for the term "San Diego dog training" you would need to have the following:

- » Google architecture compliance score of 78% or more.
- » A Google mobile compliance score that is found to be "mobile-friendly."
- » 134 pages of original content on your website (because you always want to have two times more content than your closest competition).
- » A site that loads in 3 seconds or less.
- » Relevant backlinks from reputable sites.
- » $3,000 to fix your website to get to be both architecturally and mobile compliant.
- » $26,800 to pay a search engine expert $200 per page to write 134 pages of content.
- » $75 a month for a sufficient website hosting package (Godaddy Business Hosting Grow package)

Jonathan's dog, Chauncey and the average marketing professor on most college campuses will teach about the same amount when it comes to search engine domination.

Total: $29,800

*if you paid most search engine optimization firms to optimize our website for you. However, with our system it would only cost **$4,415***

DEEP THOUGHTS FROM CLAY:

Marinate on that math for a moment... For me, this number would be very encouraging both now and when I was starting my first business out of my college dorm room. I grew up without money. When I was in college, I worked at a call center, Applebee's, Target, and as an intern at Tax and Accounting Software Company. During summers I worked well over 80 hours per week as a home health aide at night and a very low-skilled concrete construction worker during the day. Without reservation, I spent over $2,000 per month on Yellow Page advertisements and nearly $1,000 per month on bridal trade show booths while I was still in college. To afford this marketing, both my wife and I decided to live without air conditioning and to operate with only one mobile phone and one car. We made sacrifices, but they paid off. If I owned a dog training company in San Diego and I just discovered that for a total of $29,800 I could beat my competition, I would be pumped and would be asking when we could get started! The excitement of this would have me salivating like a bulldog.

I am here to help you win, but I can't do that if I don't know what search terms you are trying to win. If I were you, I would not move on from this page until you've asked our team do a free audit and evaluation of your website and until you have determined your "winnable keywords." To get the ball rolling, fill out the form at ThrivetimeShow.com/Website today.

Once you have determined your winnable keywords, it is time to begin the process of executing the proven winning strategy, which includes the following steps that we'll teach you in a minute.

JONATHAN'S
GLORIOUS BULLDOG,
"CHAUNCEY"

4 SUPER MOVES to Determine What Keywords to Optimize Your Website for:

Move 1 - Type in the search terms that YOU think your ideal and likely buyers might be searching for. As an example let's say that you think that your ideal and likely buyers might be searching for "Dallas wedding cakes." Now do a quick Google search for "Dallas wedding cakes." Don't over think this.

Move 2 - Scroll to the bottom of the search engine results and you will see "Searches related to Dallas wedding cakes." These are the keywords that YOU WANT to optimize for. But why can't it be more complicated? Because, search engine domination is not complicated, it just requires diligent consistent effort and we know that you are up to this task.

dallas wedding cakes   🎤   Q

Coffee and dessert	Birthday cakes	Best coffee	Cake shops

Searches related to wedding cakes

cake bakery dallas	champagne cake dallas
walmart wedding cakes	frosted art bakery
custom cakes dallas	elena's cakes
panini bakery dallas	dallas cakes bakeries

Move 3 - Ask your actual customers what they would actually type into the search engines to find the products and services that you offer. Do you mean that I should actually talk to another human? Isn't there an "app" for that? Yes.

Talk to an actual human. In fact talk to hundreds of humans and ask them what keywords they would actually type into search engines to find the products and services that you offer. The vast majority of people don't all search for the same keywords. In fact well over 50% of all search engine results are not "the most popular search term."

Everybody in your town doesn't search for "business coach Denver."Some people search for "America's #1 Business Coach," some people search for "who is the best business coach?", and still others search for "business coach near me."

When searching for haircuts some people search "best mens haircuts in Tulsa" or "Jenks mens haircuts" or "haircuts in jenks" etc...

Move 4 - Go to your competition's website and then simply right click on their homepage and click "view source." There you can see the keywords that your competition is focused on optimizing for. There in their actual source code you can see their "title tags," their "meta description" and their "keyword" focus. Find what is working for them and then just out work them.

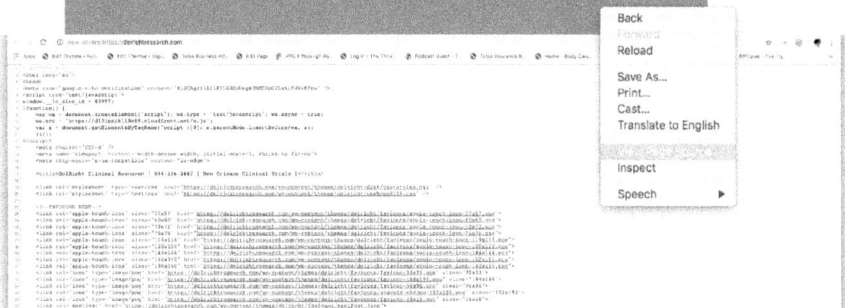

***Bonus Note - If it took you $4,415 to win a keyword, how many closed deals or in this example "dog training classes" would you need to sell in order for it to be worth it? How many sales are you missing out on by NOT being on the first page? According to Forbes, 75% of users never scroll past the first page of search results.

NOTABLE QUOTABLE

"Most people think it's all about the idea. It's not. Everyone has ideas... The hard part is to execute on the idea."

- MARK CUBAN

(The iconic entrepreneur and NBA basketball team owner of the Dallas Mavericks)

NOTABLE QUOTABLE

"Simple can be harder than complex. You have to work hard to get your thinking clean to make it simple."

- STEVE JOBS

(Co-founder of Apple, the former CEO of PIXAR, and the founder of NeXT.)

"Luck is what happens when Preparation meets opportunity." - Seneca

(Famous roman stoic philosopher, dramatist, and statesman)

SUCCESS STORIES 🏆

"We began with very few leads. So what's happening? We've doubled our incoming leads."

- CHRIS DE JESUS

(Owner of Breakout Creative)
- See their success at BreakoutCreativeCompany.)

BREAKOUT CREATIVE!

SUCCESS STORIES 🏆

"When we started, if you put my name in exactly spelled correctly, you might've found me on 20 pages back. So, we started from scratch and now we're climbing the Google search engine each day. That's a nice, new thing. People come in and are like, "Hey, I saw you online. Literally, from a year and a half ago to now, we're up double."

- DR. BRECK KASBAUM

(Founder of Dr. Breck Kasbaum Chiropractor
- See his success at www.DrBreck.com)

SUCCESS STORIES 🏆

"Clay taught me how to put a website together, how to optimize the website, how to blog, and how to use social media because we had an old school website and I think we got maybe 50 website visits a month. And then once we improved our website as part of the business coaching for bridal shops program from Clay, we started getting more calls and more calls. And I mean, I think our highest number so far has been up in 3,000s and we get more people walking in. Obviously the more customers that we can speak with, the more people we can sell our product to. I believe that the training that you get here is going to be the best money spent."

- JENNIFER THOMPSON

(Founder of Facchianos Bridal
- See her success at Facchianos.com)

NOTABLE QUOTABLE

"I have been impressed with the urgency of doing. Knowing is not enough; we must apply. Being willing is not enough; we must do. "

- LEONARDO DA VINCI

(An epic polymath who taught himsef to be a master at invention, drawing, painting, sculpting, and more.)

CHAPTER 2

ULTIMATE SEARCH ENGINE DOMINATION CHECKLIST

In order for you to achieve total SEARCH ENGINE DOMINATION and DRAMATICALLY increase your level of COMPENSATION you must simply check off and complete all of the checklist items on this website evaluation. We humbly refer to this checklist as "The Ultimate Search Engine Domination Checklist."

The Ultimate Search Engine DOMINATION Checklist
(and Website Evaluation):

_____ **Host your website with a reliable hosting service**. If your website is hosted with an unreliable hosting service you will rank lower in the search engines. We recommend using GoDaddy.com. Don't host your website with some local, janky hosting provider who lives with his mom in the basement.

_____ **Host your website with the fastest package that you can afford.** Google REALLY CARES about how long it takes for your website to load. Why? Because people get impatient and will quickly move on to another website if your website takes too long to load. On January 17th of 2018, Google formally announced the "Speed Update." Google's plan called for them to slowly roll out the new search engine ranking criteria to give web-developers plenty of time to make their websites load much, much faster. To test the speed of your website visit: https://developers.google.com/speed/pagespeed/insights/ To read more about Google's new speed requirements visit: https://www.forbes.com/sites/jaysondemers/2018/01/29/will-googles-new-page-speed-criteria-affect-your-site/#396634ed6a8f

____ **Build your website on the WordPress platform.** "WordPress offers the best out-of-the-box search engine optimization imaginable." - Tim Ferriss (Best-selling author of *The 4-Hour Work Week*, *The 4-Hour Body*, *The 4-Hour Chef*, *Tools of Titans,* and *Tribe of Mentors*. He is also an early stage investor in Facebook, Twitter, Evernote, Uber, etc.)

Don't use any other website building platform than WordPress. If you hire coders to custom build your website on PHP or .NET you will end up hating your life as a result of having a website that nobody can update other than the entitled, nefarious employees who now have the ability to hold you hostage. Trust us here. We have personally coached hundreds of clients and every time our coaching clients have a custom built website the business owner at some point has been held hostage by the employee who is the only person who knows how to update the custom built, non-search engine friendly, and ridiculously complicated website. Building your website on WordPress puts the power back in your hands as a business owner because you can update the website yourself if you have to.

PRO TIP: USE WORDPRESS.ORG NOT WORDPRESS.COM

WordPress.org is the open source platform used to power the best SEO compliant websites in the world. WordPress.com is their platform that does not allow for plugins or optimal website optimization.

*Avoid WordPress.com

____ **Build a mobile-friendly website.** What is a mobile friendly website? Check your website's mobile compliance at: https://search.google.com/test/mobile-friendly. If this link changes in the future just search for "Google mobile compliance test" in the Google search engine and you'll find it.

_____ Install HTTPS encryption onto your website.
HTTPS encryption stands for Hypertext Transfer Protocol
Secure. What does that mean? HTTPS encryption makes
your website more difficult for bad people to hack, thus
making it tougher for very bad people to crash your
website and to use your website as a way to steal the
personal information of your valuable clients and patrons.
Google ranks websites higher who have invested the
additional money needed to add HTTPS encryption to
their website. How many times would you use Google if
every time their search results sent you to websites that
had been hacked into by cyber criminals and internet
hackers?

← → C ⌂   🔒(https)/www.youtube.com

**_____Install the Yoast.com search engine optimization
plugin into your website.** What is Yoast? Yoast SEO is
the best WordPress plugin on the planet when it comes
to search engine optimization. Yoast was built and
designed in a way to make search engine optimization
approachable for everyone, and thus we love Yoast.
Yoast makes it possible for people who are not complete
nerds to proactively manage the search engine
optimization of their website.

DEFINITION MAGICIAN
Plugin - A plugin is a piece of code or software that provides a
variety of functions that you can add to your WordPress website.
Plugins allow you to increase the functional capacity of your website
without having to hire a bunch of nefarious, entitled custom coders
who are typically hard to manage because you do not have any idea
what they are working on or what they are talking about 90% of the
time.

____Uniquely optimize every meta title tag on every page of your website.
The title tag is simply a hypertext markup language (HTML) element on a website that specifies to search engines what a particular web page is all about. "according to SEOMoz, the best practice for the title tag length is to keep titles under 70 characters." An example would be, "Full Package Media | Dallas Real Estate Photography | 972-885-8823"

Full Package Media | Dallas Real Estate Photography | 972-885-8823
https://fullpackagemedia.com/.
Looking for the best in the business when it comes to Dallas Real Estate Photography? You need to

____Uniquely optimize every meta description on every page of your website. The meta description is simply part of the hypertext markup language (HTML) code that provides a brief summary about a web page. Search engines like Google usually show the meta description in search engine results. Don't make your meta descriptions more than 160 characters in length.

An ample example would be, "Looking for the best in the business when it comes to Dallas Real Estate Photography? You need to call Full Package Media today at 972-885-8823."

Looking for the best in the business when it comes to Dallas Real Estate Photography? You need to call Full Package Media today at 972-885-8823.
Careers About Us Contact Us Client Login

____Uniquely optimize the keywords on every page of your website. Meta keywords are a very specific kind of meta tag that will show up in the hypertext markup language (HTML) code on web pages and these will tell the search engines what the web page is really all about. An example of specific keyword optimization would be "Berj Najarian." You may be thinking, who is Berj Najarian?

Berj Najarian serves as the New England Patriots Director of Football and the "Chief of Staff" for the legendary Coach Bill Belichick who has won a total of 8 Super Bowl titles since beginning his coaching career in the National Football League. If someone is searching for "Berj Najarian" there is a high probability that they already know who "Berj Najarian" is and if you want to rank high in the search engines when people are searching for "Berj Najarian" you definitely want to make sure that you have declared your meta keyword phrase as "Berj Najarian."

Quick Note: If at any point while reading this you are beginning to feel overwhelmed just submit your website for an audit and deep dive evaluation and we'll do the heavy lifting for you. You can submit your website to be audited at: www.ThrivetimeShow.com/Website

_____ **Create 1,000 words of original and relevant text (content) per page on your website.** Are we saying that somebody actually has to write, 1,000 original words of original and relevant text for every page of your website? Yes. Isn't there a hack? NO. Can't there be a better way? No.

Can't you just go out and hire a company out of India to use "spinners" to slightly change existing text for you? NO. Can't you just copy content from another website? NO.

You can spend every minute of every day trying to find some blogger or some website experts out there that will tell you that someone on your team doesn't need to invest the time needed to create 1,000 words of both original and relevant content and you will eventually find them and they will be 100% wrong. However, they will gladly take your money.

PERMALINK

META TITLE TAG

META DESCRIPTION

YOU OR A MEMBER OF YOUR TEAM MUST WRITE 1,000 WORDS OF ORIGINAL AND RELEVANT CONTENT FOR EVERY PAGE OF YOUR WEBSITE.

_____ **Create a Google search engine compliant .XML sitemap on your website.** What is an .XML sitemap? XML stands for Extensible Markup Language. A quality XML sitemap serves as a map of your website which allows the Google search engine to find all of the important pages located within your website. As a website owner unless you hate money, you REALLY WANT GOOGLE to be able to crawl (find, rank, and sort) all of the important pages on your website. Yoast.com has tools that will actually generate Google compliant .XML sitemaps for you. Don't worry, you can do this!

Fun Fact: I had to take Algebra 3 times en route to getting into Oral Roberts University and I was eventually kicked out of college for writing a parody about the school's president "ORU Slim Shady" which you can currently find on YouTube. If I can learn and master search engine optimization you can too!

HTML

_____**Create a Google search engine compliant HTML sitemap.** What's an HTML site map? A hypertext markup language sitemap allows the people who visit your website to easily navigate your website. This sitemap should be located at the bottom of your website and should be labeled as a "Sitemap."

Hiding your sitemap for any reason is a bad idea because Google assumes that if you are hiding your sitemap you are probably trying to hide something. Don't change the background of your website to be the same color as your sitemap's font or do anything tricky here. You want to make sure that your website's sitemap can easily be found at the bottom of your website. See the example below:

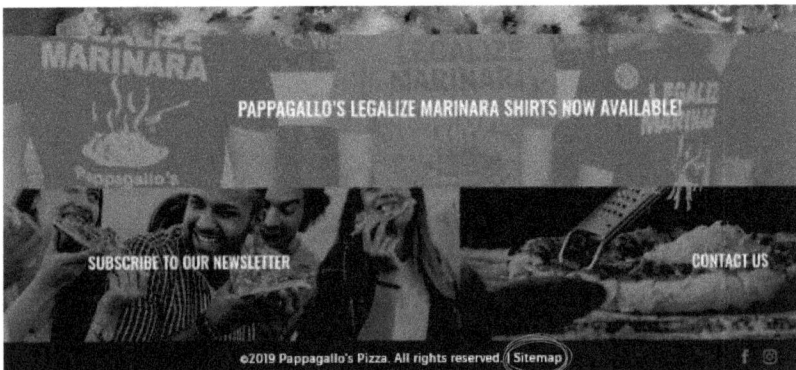

_____**Create a clickable phone number.** If you ever want to sell something to humans on the planet Earth you must make your contact information easy to find. Thus you want to make your phone number easily available to find at either the top right or at the bottom of your website. When coaching your web-developer, force them to make your phone number a "click-to-call" phone number so that users on your website who are using a mobile phone (almost everyone) can simply click the number to call you.

In our shameless attempt to make this the BEST, MOST
HUMBLE and the MOST ACTIONABLE SEARCH
ENGINE OPTIMIZATION book of all time we have
provided the following real examples from REAL
clients just like you who we have really helped to
REALLY increase their REAL sales year after year:

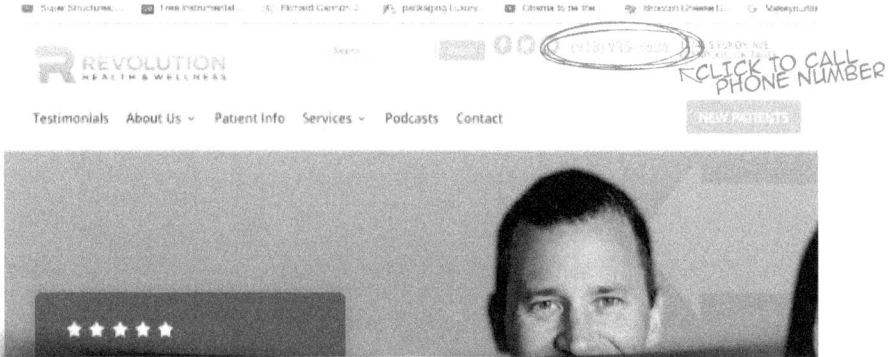

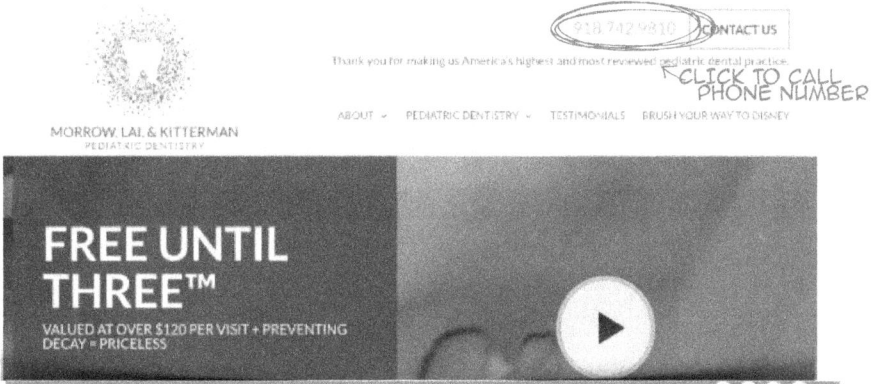

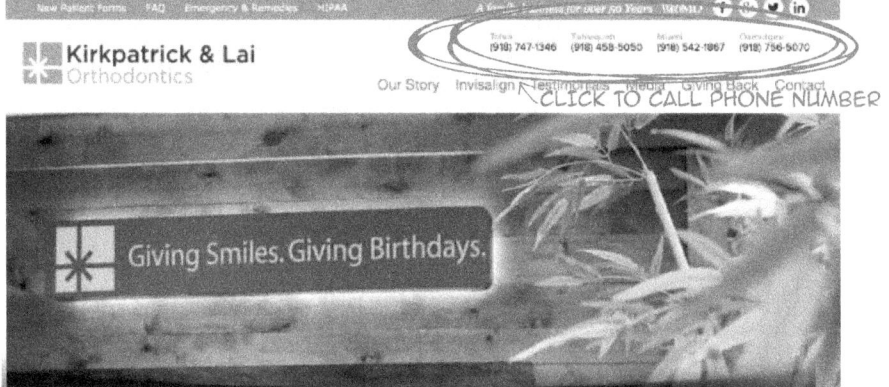

_____**Have a Social Proof.** If you don't hate money and you are not a committed socialist, you will want to include some social proof near the top of your website. What is social proof? "Social proof" is a phrase and a term that was original created by the best-selling author Robert Cialdini in his book, **Influence**. The best social proof examples are:

a. Real testimonials from real current and former clients is super powerful.

b. Media features and appearances on credible media sources like Bloomberg, Fox Business, Entrepreneur.com, Fast Company, etc.

c. Proudly showing that you have earned the highest and most reviews in your local business niche.

d. Celebrity endorsements from celebrities that have earned the trust of your ideal and likely buyers.

e. Listed below is an example that will showcase to you what it looks like to use social proof effectively.

_____**Make the logo return to home.** Allow the logo on your website to serve as your "homepage" button. As of 2019, most people assume that if they click your logo they are going to be taken back to the homepage of your website.

_____**Create original content.** You must create more original and relevant content than anyone else in the world about your specific search engine focus. If you want to come up top in the world for the phrase "organic supplements" you must then create the most original and relevant content on the planet about "organic supplements." If you want to come up top in your city for the phrase "knee pain Tulsa" then you must what? You must create the most original and relevant content on the planet about "knee pain Tulsa."

If you want to come up top in the search engine results for the phrase "America's #1 business coach" then you must create the most original and relevant content on the planet about "America's #1 business coach." Listed below are a few examples of receiving high search rankings due to having the most original, relevant content on the planet about that particular subject.

america's #1 business coach

All   News   Images   Videos   Maps   More   Settings   Tools

About 5,870,000 results (0.35 seconds)

Business Coach | Bill Belichick's #1 Fan and America's #1 Business ...
https://www.thrivetimeshow.com/the...show/business-coach-management-principles/ ▾
★ ★ ★ ★ ★ Rating: 99% - 2,651 votes
Bill Belichick's number one fan and America's #1 business coach Clay Clark teaches many of the successful management principles that Belichick ...

People also ask

Who is the best business coach in the world?   ⌄

What should I look for in a business coach?   ⌄

1.3 mi · 3019 E 101st St · (918) 299-4415 ext. 5384

WEBSITE   DIRECTIONS

The Little Gym of SE Tulsa
4.7 ★★★★★ (14) · Gymnastics center
3.3 mi · 6556 E 91st St · (918) 492-2626
Open · Closes 7:30PM
🌐 Their website mentions **gymnastics classes**

WEBSITE   DIRECTIONS

Twist & Shout Tumbling & Cheer
3.5 ★★★★★ (8) · Gym
6.2 mi · 4820 S 83rd E Ave · (918) 622-5867
Closed · Opens 5PM
🌐 Their website mentions **tumbling classes**

WEBSITE   DIRECTIONS

≡ More places

Tumbling Tulsa | Tulsa Tumbling Lessons | 918-764-8804
https://justicetumblingco.com/ ▾
If you are looking for the best and highest reviewed **tumbling Tulsa** place, you need to call us at Justice
Tumbling today and see what makes us better.
Services · About · Schedule · Testimonials

Tulsa Cheerleading | Tumbling Tulsa | Tulsa Tumbling | 918-986-5785
https://tumblesmart.com/ ▾
Tulsa's Most Reviewed **Tumbling** Program. **Tumble** Smart Athletics. Free Evaluation **Lesson**Meet the
Owner. **Tumbling Tulsa** Gymnast Stars. Experience the

Google   tulsa knee pain   🎤   🔍

META TITLE TAG

Tulsa Knee Pain - Revolution Health Tulsa
https://www.revolutionhealth.org/.../tulsa-knee-pain-revolution-health-is-bring-in-a-re... ▾
Find the best treatment for your **Tulsa knee pain** right here in Tulsa. Find out more about Revolution
Health by calling at 918-935-3636.

PERMALINK

META DESCRIPTION

Tulsa knee Pain | Revolution Health Oklahoma
https://www.revolutionhealth.org/.../tulsa-knee-pain-find-the-top-and-quickest-result-f... ▾
The best prolotherapy is right here at Revolution Health for **Tulsa knee pain.**

Best Prolotherapy Treatments Tulsa | Tulsa Knee Pain
https://www.revolutionhealth.org/.../tulsa-knee-pain-find-the-best-possible-tulsa-knee-... ▾
Best Of The Best Prolotherapy Treatments for your **tulsa knee Pain**

Non-invasive remedies relieve knee pain without surgery - Tulsa World
https://www.tulsaworld.com/...knee-pain.../article_6bdf681d-d017-554c-9ecc-fae529... ▾
Mar 13, 2019 - Dear Doctor K: I have osteoarthritis of the knee. Are there ways to relieve my **knee pain**
without drugs or surgery?

_____**Create a "Testimonials," "Case Studies," or a "Success Stories" portion of your website** if you want to sell something to humans who were not born yesterday. Most shoppers today have become savvy and are aware of the fact that great companies generate great reviews (and occasionally bad ones) and that bad companies chronically generate bad reviews (and occasionally some good ones). Thus, most people will want to actually see testimonials, case studies or success stories from real clients that have actually worked with your company in the past.

In fact, not having testimonials, case studies, and success stories on your website freaks most people out to the point that they won't even call you or fill out your contact form.

How do we know this? Well, for starters, we are humans who happen to be also consumers and Forbes tells us that, "Almost 90% of consumers said they read reviews for local businesses. In other words, if you are not investing efforts into online reputation management, then you are missing out on having control of the first impression your business has." - *Online Reviews and Their Impact On the Bottom* Line by Matt Bowman - https://www.forbes.com/sites/forbesagencycouncil/2019/01/15/online-reviews-and-their-impact-on-the-bottom-line/#35d3b4955bde

NOTABLE QUOTABLE

"Perfectionism is often an excuse for procrastination."

- PAUL GRAHAM
(The entrepreneur investor, incubator, and coach behind AirBNB, Dropbox, and Reddit)

_____**Include a compelling 60-second video / commercial (on the top portion above the fold) on your website** to improve your conversion rate. To provide you with an ample example of clients that we have personally worked with who have used a "website header video" in route to dramatically increasing their sales check out:

VIDEO PLAY BUTTON

_____**Create a "top of the website" call to action** that your ideal and likely buyers will relate to and connect with. You want to make it SUPER EASY for your ideal and likely buyers to call you, to schedule an appointment with you, or for them to do business with you in the most convenient way possible. As an AMPLE EXAMPLE check out EITRLounge.com and OXIFresh.com:

CALL TO ACTION

CALL TO ACTION

_____ **Create a "No-Brainer" sales offer deal** that is so GOOD, so HOT, and so IRRESISTIBLE that your ideal and likely buyers simply cannot resist the urge to at least try out your services and products out. As an example, we would encourage you to check out the following websites.

NOTABLE QUOTABLE

"Genius is 1% inspiration and 99% perspiration."

- THOMAS EDISON
(The inventor of the first practical light bulb, recorded audio, recorded video, and the founder of General Electric)

SUCCESS STORIES 🏆

"Being top in Google has impacted our business tremendously. Knowing that we're top in Google makes it so much easier for our clients to search and if they use certain keywords that pertain to our business, we're the first ones that come up on that page. We get a lot of phone call and website traffic. I would suggest every one takes this program seriously."

- MYRON KIRKPATRICK
(Founder of White Glove Auto - WhiteGloveAutoTulsa.com)

"WHEN I WAS 5 YEARS OLD, MY MOTHER ALWAYS TOLD ME THAT HAPPINESS WAS THE KEY TO LIFE. WHEN I WENT TO SCHOOL, THEY ASKED ME WHAT I WANTED TO BE WHEN I GREW UP. I WROTE DOWN 'HAPPY'. THEY TOLD ME I DID NOT UNDERSTAND THE ASSIGNMENT, AND I TOLD THEM THEY DID NOT UNDERSTAND LIFE."

John Lennon

(An English singer and songwriter who became internationally famous as a member and co-founder of the Beatles)

ABOUT THE AUTHORS

Clay Clark (@TheClayClark):

Clay is the former U.S. SBA Entrepreneur of the Year and the founder of Thrive15.com. Over the course of his career, he has been a founding team member of many companies including www. DJConnection.com, www.EITRLounge.com, www.EpicPhotos.com, www.MakeYourLifeEpic.com, Tip Top K9 Franchises, and more. He and his companies have been featured in Forbes, Fast Company, Entrepreneur, PandoDaily, Bloomberg TV, Bloomberg Radio, the Entrepreneur's On Fire Podcast, the So Money Podcast with Farnoosh Torabi and on countless media outlets. He's been the speaker of choice of Hewlett-Packard, Maytag University, O'Reilly Auto Parts, Valspar Paint, Farmers Insurance and countless other companies.

He is the father of choice for his and his wife Vanessa's five kids and is the proud owner of 24 chickens and 13 cats. Clay is an obsessive New England Patriots fan and Tim Tebow apologist. He wears a baseball jersey every day and enjoys reading business case studies and autobiographies about successful entrepreneurs when not chasing his kids and his wife around.

Dr. Timothy Johnson, MD

Dr. Tim Johnson, MD is an ophthalmologist in Alabama. He was born in Tuscaloosa, AL – Roll Tide. He attended Birmingham-Southern College in Birmingham, AL for his undergraduate education, where he graduated valedictorian and Phi Beta Kappa. He then attended Emory University School of Medicine in Atlanta, GA for his medical education, where he graduated Alpha Omega Alpha. He then attended the prestigious Wills Eye Hospital in Philadelphia, PA for his ophthalmology training.

He first learned organizational and time management/ entrepreneurial skills in medical school when he served as a Howard Hughes Medical Institute research fellow and managed a research team of over two dozen post-doctoral, medical school, and undergraduate students to present and publish over 100 peer-reviewed journal articles, book chapters, and presentations. His research achievements include discovering a novel vein in the human body, being the first to capture on video actively bleeding iris microhemangiomatosis, creating the electronic International Prostate Symptom Score, and creating an award-winning medical device. He still conducts medical research, investigating the impact of anxiety on clinical metrics of outpatient cataract surgery.

Following his medical training, he began working with his father, Dr. E Van Johnson, MD at Tuscaloosa Ophthalmology. Soon after, he founded Southern Eye Consultants, a referral eye surgery clinic, and caught the medical entrepreneurship bug. He recently founded Freedom Ophthalmology, a refractive clinic that supports FightfortheForgotten.org.

HIS FAVORITE QUOTES INCLUDE:

"THE MOST DIFFICULT THING IS THE DECISION TO ACT, THE REST IS MERELY TENACITY. THE FEARS ARE PAPER TIGERS. YOU CAN DO ANYTHING YOU DECIDE TO DO."

Amelia Earhart

(American aviation pioneer who became the first woman to fly solo across the Atlantic Ocean)

"LEAP AND THE NET WILL APPEAR."

John Burroughs

(Naturalist and essayist, friend to Thomas Edison, Walt Whitman, Theodore Roosevelt)

WANT TO LEARN MORE SO THAT YOU CAN EARN MORE?

THROUGHOUT THE YEARS CLAY HAS
WRITTEN THE FOLLOWING BOOKS.

START HERE
The World's Best Business Growth & Consulting Book: Business Growth Strategies from the World's Best Business Coach

DON'T LET YOUR EMPLOYEES HOLD YOU HOSTAGE
This candid book shares how to avoid being held hostage by employees.

F6 JOURNAL
Meta Thrive Time Journal

THE ENTREPRENEUR'S DRAGON ENERGY
The Mindset Kanye, Trump and You Need to Succeed

BOOM
The 13 Proven Steps to Business Success

MAKE YOUR LIFE EPIC
Clay shares his journey and struggle from the dorm room to the board room during his raw and action-packed story of how he built DJConnection.com.

JACKASSARY
Jackassery will serve as a beacon of light for other entrepreneurs that are looking to avoid troublesome employees and difficult situations. This is real. This is raw. This is unfiltered entrepreneurship.

THE ART OF GETTING THINGS DONE
Clay Clark breaks down the proven, time-tested and time freedom creating super moves that you can use to create both the time freedom and financial freedom that most people only dream about.

THRIVE
How to Take Control of Your Destiny and Move Beyond Surviving... Now!

WILL NOT WORK FOR FOOD
9 Big Ideas for Effectively Managing Your Business in an Increasingly Dumb, Distracted & Dishonest America

WHEEL OF WEALTH
An Entrepreneur's Action Guide

BECOMING THE ELEPHANT IN THE ROOM
57 Words of Wisdom and Mindsets to Becoming a Successful Person